14.99

CHASING COOL

EXAMINING THE PURSUITS OF YOUR HEART

BRETT RICKEY

BEACON HILL PRESS
OF KANSAS CITY

ISBN 978-0-8341-2324-3

Printed in the
United States of America

Cover Design: Chad A Cherry
Interior Design: Sharon Page

Library of Congress Cataloging-in-Publication Data

Rickey, Brett, 1963-
Chasing cool : examining the pursuits of your heart / Brett Rickey.
p. cm.
Includes bibliographical references.
ISBN-13: 978-0-8341-2324-3 (pbk.)
ISBN-10: 0-8341-2324-X (pbk.)
1. Youth—Religious life. 2. Spirituality. I. Title.

BV4531.3.R53 2007
248.8'3—dc22

2007024369

10 9 8 7 6 5 4 3 2 1

CONTENTS

INTRODUCTION

I'm a child of the church. From day one I grew up as a preacher's kid and have known a very blessed life with a pair of godly parents who still pray for me every day. For that I'm extremely grateful.

But as a pastor's kid in church, I was forced to sit through more than my desired number of worship services. And since my mind was a lot like yours, during preaching my thoughts tended to wander. No disrespect to my dad—he's still a great preacher, but there were days I just wasn't into listening. So my friends and I would write notes or whisper during church when any topic stirred within us that was semirelevant to spiritual matters. (I figured if I was going to *talk* in church, it had better be "spiritual.") So we would mark time by asking each other wacky questions about hypothetical situations.

Like many in my day, the Second Coming was a hot topic after the publication of Hal Lindsey's book *The Late Great Planet Earth*. Along with that every church in the United States scared the stuffing out of its teens with the movie *A Thief in the Night* and the famous song "I Wish We'd All Been Ready." So my friends and I would sit around discussing big questions such as, "What if Jesus really did come back, right now?" This led me to the grown-up questions, "Am I ever going to get married and have kids?" "And what if Jesus came back right when I was getting married, at what moment would I be legally wed?" Those are the questions of life. Here's another hypothetical—just for fun. "If a brown cow from Germany and a black cow from Russia were to both live in the same field, both eating green grass and drinking semitransparent water, what color would their milk be?"

Hypothetical situations take us into a world that has not happened—into a world that may never happen but could. Here's one we can try on for size. "What would happen in Arlington, Texas, if the Texas Rangers were to win the World Series?" (Notice a hypothetical situation doesn't have to be plausible in reality, just in fantasy, as my Rangers have yet to advance to the big dance.) Would there be looting and gunfire or just a simple parade attended by the mayor driving a new Mustang GT convertible? To answer that question is to engage the imagination and travel into a world of the not yet.

As I was writing this, the United States Supreme Court argued its first case with Chief Justice John Roberts presiding. The case was a lightning rod issue for Roberts from the start, because it involved the parental notification laws that are on the books in New Hampshire concerning abortion. Apparently the lawmakers up there are a bit stodgy and feel that parents should have to consent if their darling minor daughters decide to have an abortion—which, when you consider it, may be a little strict, don't you think? (I say that in jest.) All the Supreme Court arguments that day were made in the realm of the hypothetical, since the law has yet to go into effect. It was strange to hear all those smart people talk about things that hadn't happened *but could.* They have really good imaginations at the Supreme Court, even though they have to wear those dark robes.

OK, hang on—I do have a point. The hypothetical that got this book in gear was a simple one. *If a person were a Christian and lived in our culture, would it be possible for him or her to succumb to the same temptations that tripped up God's people in the Old Testament? And if that were possible, what kind of things would cause that to happen?*

As I rolled this around in my head, I started thinking out loud and observing the behaviors of our culture. I gave a talk or two on my findings, and my good friend Andy said, "Pastor, that needs to be in a book," which is what I was thinking too. I had never written a book and didn't know if it would ever see print, but the urge to write it was pretty strong.

So the result is what follows. You're reading a book about a search for truth that I'm currently on. It's a search that peers deeply into areas pastors may not want to talk about because they're all too common in our churches. The writing is light in tone, mainly because I don't like to stay serious for very long—but truth runs deep. I believe this book will give you a chance to reexamine your future. I hope it causes you to ask the hypothetical, "If I keep going down this road I'm on in life, what will become of my hopes and dreams?" My prayer is that you'll engage your imagination as we take a look at many of my own experiences and failures and how they helped me see the light to take me down a better path.

So don't stop yet—the fun is about to begin.

THE "IT" FACTOR

"They chased after other gods" (Judg. 2:12, NLT).

One of the humbling lessons that all of us learn in school somewhere along the line is that there's always somebody tougher, meaner, and even grouchier than you are. For me, the lesson was especially painful.

I was in fifth grade, and the game was kickball. I was a pretty good athlete and the cleanup hitter (kicker) in every kickball gathering. If I were to play kickball today, no doubt it would be said of me, "He's got game." A wise man once warned, "Pride goes before . . . a fall" (Prov. 16:18), and my fall was about to take place in front of the whole fifth grade at recess.

It was cold.

I don't remember her name—I just remember her size. We would now call her big boned. She had long black hair in a pony tail and always wore ball caps and other boy accessories. For you visual learners, let's just call her Big Becky. As you may know, most fifth grade big-boned girls are taller and bigger than most of the boys. She was the pitcher, and she stared in at me with benignly soft eyes that hid the menacing truth within. As she rolled the ball toward home, I ran up and nearly missed it, weakly grounding it straight to her. We raced to first, and she easily tagged me out.

Without much effort, Big Becky had wounded something deep inside of me. Evil thoughts began to disturb me. Oh, the humanity of being tagged out by a girl. My pride was damaged, and something had to be done!

It was wet.

Did I mention that it had rained the night before?

Well, that's an important visual I need to tell you, because on our playground all the bases had puddles around them after the rain, and since first base got used the most, it had the biggest puddle.

In my anger I chose to sin. I saw the water, and without thinking, my foot came up and left the ground and came down with an angled descent to make sure the water flew straight at the perpetrator of this heinous act of skullduggery—Big Becky.

The mud flew up and covered her head to toe. Bull's-eye! Vindication was now complete. A surge of short-lived pride was about to be mine—or so I thought.

Now, I'm not sure what I expected to happen next, but the worst was still to come. Did I mention that Becky was big? As quickly as the mud was on her, she was on top of me, physically, like a duck on a june bug. She had me pinned with both arms straining underneath her knees. My biceps felt as if they were being crushed, and there was no way, let me repeat, *no way* to shake free. I felt like the witch in *The Wizard of Oz* who got flattened by Dorothy's house. The air was out of my balloon. Becky was big, and she only had to say two words. They are words that still haunt me to this day. They were kindly stated in her customary fashion with no anger or hatred. They were said with a confident assurance that if I didn't answer correctly, there would be more pain to come. She said the words that no boy ever wants to hear from a girl on any playground. "You give?" she cried out. A brief silence followed.

Oh, the pain. My sluggish answer wheezed out, "Uh-huh." With her point made, she helped me up, and I walked into the school toward the nurse's office. I began to do the "loser's limp" thing and fake an injury so that my humiliation would somehow be justified. But my male friends understood what was at stake, and they knew my trauma was more than physical. They had never wanted to tangle with Big Becky either, and my experience helped seal their total respect for our female adversary. Big Becky became a legend that day, and I dropped back to the middle of the pack. You learn a lot about life on playgrounds.

Growing up on the playground, another one of the first games all of us learn is called tag. You know the rules. The person who is "it" chases down and attempts to touch those who are playing. Everybody runs from the "it" person as though he or she has a dangerous yet somehow fun disease. (All of us have faked an injury at least once so that we could be "it.") Just one touch from the "it" person makes the next person "it." And the chase continues and goes back and forth until everybody gets tired—which, at my current age, could mean before the game begins. I guess that explains why adults in my neighborhood don't play tag much anymore.

I don't know the origin of the game tag, but I do know that it's a lot like real life in reverse. Think about how we "do life" in our Western culture. The general public, including us, identify a few "it" people. But now, instead of running *from* them we chase *after* them. We buy their clothes, wear their hairstyles, and sift through their private lives hoping that somehow we possess what it takes to be "it." We follow their advice on everything from style to sex and marriage. We imitate their language and take all that they say as new truth to be learned and lived by. They're "it."

Charles Colson observes that "we are like people trying to go up the down escalator. We huff and puff and go nowhere. The problem is, the culture is pushing one way, and we haven't figured out it's the wrong direction. When we ask the basic questions about our purpose and meaning, we receive false answers."[1]

Here's what I see going on all around us in my world. Tag is still the game of choice; but the rules have changed. Now, everybody is doing the chasing, and nobody can really decide who it is that is "it." At least nobody can agree. And at my age, that kind of chase can lead to a lot of huffing and puffing.

As I thought about this whole social phenomenon,

like a world playing tag in reverse, I began to reflect on what the "it" factor was in the first place. I knew it wasn't just a particular person, because the "it" people seemed to change more often than the weather in my native Oklahoma. "It" could not be defined as a person.

Then I thought that maybe the "it" factor that people chased for was happiness. But then I observed that the celebrities that most people chased after lacked happiness, at least from our vantage point. In fact, the happiest people in the world seem to be the ones that others are least likely to imitate.

So what was the "it" factor? I believe the "it" is more attitude than personality. It has more to do with conformity than with character. In fact, more than ever, I am convinced that most people in our culture pursue this from their earliest days in grade school without even being aware of it. The "it" I am talking about is the four-letter word *cool.* Cool!

On the surface, at first glance, you might be thinking, "Well, so what? Everybody wants to be a little cool, to fit in and not be a nerd or a geek. And there isn't a commandment against trying to be cool." True enough. In fact, many unwitting church people think that being uncool is the path to being like Jesus. If that's you, I'm sorry. Jesus was the coolest person in His day, which I'll talk about more a little later.

The truth is you don't have to be uncool to be a Christ follower. But to be a Christ follower, you must follow Christ. And when Christ and cool conflict, Christ's path must win. But there's the rub I see in Western Christianity. Cool seems to win too often, even in the church among people who profess to be Christ followers. When cool and Christ go head-to-head, cool is holding its own.

But we aren't doing anything that new after all. Many generations have preceded us in this pursuit, though it has been called by different names.

While reading the Old Testament, I noticed the similarities to my world today. And it's my desire to point out that God's people today face the same temptations as those before. The only difference is in the packaging.

Three things stand out to me in the following short passage that will help us explore our connection to the people of Israel. Their history shows that they missed God's best, and this passage is a foreshadowing of things that would plague them forever.

Notice what they chased:

> Then Joshua son of Nun, the servant of the LORD, died at the age of 110. . . . After that generation died, another generation grew up who did not acknowledge the LORD or remember the mighty

> things he had done for Israel. Then the Israelites did what was evil in the LORD's sight and worshiped the images of Baal. They abandoned the LORD, the God of their ancestors, who had brought them out of Egypt. *They chased after other gods,* worshiping the gods of the people around them. And they angered the LORD. They abandoned the LORD to serve Baal *(Judg. 2:8, 10-13, NLT, emphasis added).*

Here are a few of the things that God has shown me from this passage. First, *every generation must experience God for itself.* Joshua, Israel's mighty leader, had just died, and so had all the people he influenced directly. He was a radical follower of God, and his example was copied by God's people. Joshua's generation had seen the Jordan River stop flowing as the ark of the covenant was carried across. The river was at flood stage, but God had held the waters back so that the people of Israel could enter the Promised Land. Joshua's generation had seen the walls of Jericho smash to the ground as a result of the thunderous power of praise of God Almighty. They didn't even have to throw a rock to win that fight. They had seen God help them defeat enemies that seemed unbeatable. They had watched God keep His promises as they did their part in fighting the good fight. But now all of these faithful ones were dead and gone. Their children now had control of the ship. And the children had a different view of success in life. They decided that the nations all around them were having a lot more fun than they were. Their pagan worship involved a lot more sensuality, and a lot less holy living and all those rules. They failed to experience God for themselves, but instead they relied on a secondhand experience by way of Joshua and his leadership. Once he was gone, so was their faith.

Second, *every generation is capable of memory loss.* Look at that phrase—they didn't "remember the mighty things he had done for Israel." In the good old U.S.A., these words could be used to describe the media and pop culture when looking back at our Christian roots as a nation. Most people alive today think we are a blessed nation because of our democratic form of government. They have failed to acknowledge, or just don't understand, that the hand of God may have helped bring our nation to a place of power in the world so that we could be agents of good. Our nation and government were founded by people who shared a belief in a Creator who is able and willing to act on behalf of His people, not that every one of them were saints. But people just seem to forget.

Closer to home, I have seen families saved from the ravages of drug addiction. They head out on the right path for a while, following Christ, but something doesn't stick. Old friends and old hangouts come back out of nowhere. They relapse, and they forget. The Israelites forgot, and so do we. Every generation is capable of memory loss.

Third, *every generation will chase after something.* Verse 12 holds the key to why I wrote this book in the first place, "They abandoned the LORD, the God of their ancestors, who had brought them out of Egypt. They chased after other gods, worshiping the gods of the people around them" (NLT).

Right now, if you own this book, I want you to underline those words *chased after others gods.* It's the big idea for the rest of this chapter. Israel got caught in a game of reverse tag. And the "it" person for them wasn't a person at all. It was a god named Baal. And if you know anything at all about your Old Testament, this god would be a major pain in their historical neck.

So look at the god they chased. Its name was Baal. Baal was an idol or statue that you could put on your coffee table at home, carved out of wood, stone, or some kind of metal. Not very impressive, I know. And as a kid, I could never understand why the Israelites would be so stupid.

But without going into too much detail, let me say that Baal worship was really a lot different from just bowing down to a carved figurine. Baal was a fertility

God, and it was his job to send the rain. But when you worshiped Baal, the intrigue of lust and sexuality was involved. A man could go to a "high place" of Baal worship and consort with a prostitute as an act of worship. As one of my college professors once stated, "You didn't need a bus ministry for Baal worship."[2] The men would be there without much of a fight. Also, when you could carve an image and call it a god, you could make it do what you wanted it to do. The image was there to bring comfort and symbolize the hope that a spiritual being was helping you out. And since the Baal image was a god of fertility, the belief was that by worshiping Baal in the right manner, you could show Baal what he needed to do. He needed to bring rain and make sure that the crops grew like they should and that all the animals had big families.

Comedian Arsenio Hall in the 1980s had a bit during his late-night show that he called "things that make you go hmm." Here's one for you. Notice the similarities between Baal and another four-letter word I used earlier? Consonant, double vowel, followed by an L. Hmm—sound familiar? Kind of like a word found in the title of this book. C-o-o-l, maybe? Coincidence? Hmm.

Baal worship is not really that big anymore, but the idol it represents is still alive in the modern idol of cool. *Cool is an image.* I believe, or as my granny would say, "I'm here to tell ya" that the attitude of cool has in fact become an idol. Growing up, I heard pastors refer to big cars and fat wallets as idols. But idols in modern times are not just things. Idols can be ideas you worship in place of God. Something you chase . . . something that captures your heart that shouldn't.

Now before you toss the book, I have nothing against the word *cool. Cool* is a word I use dozens of times every day. *Cool* as a word is not in itself good or bad. It's a descriptive word that I can say about a lot of things. For instance, if somebody shows me a slick mail piece with good graphics, I say, "That looks cool." If I see a tricked-out chopper on the road, I say, "Wow—that is cool!" *Cool* is a cool word. There's nothing wrong with the word.

But it's the pursuit of cool that worries me. I am convinced that the majority of people you meet on the streets, regardless of their status or income or years in life, are chasing this god of our age. I mean, really, look at most of the people who ride Harleys. Give it up! Seriously, though, any of us are susceptible to the temptation of chasing cool. I also believe that chasing cool is the primary cause of the powerlessness in the Church in America.

Since the pursuit of cool is on my hot list, you may ask, what is cool anyway? Let's make it a stop-and-think question. So what comes to your mind when you think of the word *cool*? I think it’s something different for each person. Who decides what cool is? Cool people? Who are the cool people? Depends on who you ask, doesn’t it? Why does cool keep moving? Things that were cool when I was a kid aren’t cool now, not even close. I have a canary-yellow leisure suit picture from Easter, circa 1974. Yellow leisure suits will not be cool again anytime soon—if *ever* again!

I remember the exclamations “far out!” and “I’m hip to your jive” as being cool at some time in my life. Are some things cool longer than others?

So who is the judge of cool? Since everyone tries to find it, there must be somebody that is keeping score.

Are you cool? How would you know? If you say you are cool, is that being uncool? What does cool cost? Is it free, just innate, or does it cost something? Well, these are the questions I have when thinking about the word *cool*.

So who decides what’s cool? I guess we all do, in some way. But as soon as anyone grasps it, it vanishes like smoke. I recall an album cover picture from decades ago where comedian Steve Martin is wearing an arrow through his head. It was cool then, but my 14-year-old daughter wouldn’t even smile if she saw it today. So who are the cool people? Nobody fully agrees, but we do have our top 40 lists and our magazines filled with the "most beautiful people."

And we sure like to dress like and look like those thought to be cool. Britney Spears has a clothing line and a new perfume. (My daughter tells me that it smells great.) Britney's cool factor is currently sliding due to the birth and reported neglect of her first child. Celebrity endorsements for everything from Taco Bell to electric razors continue to entice us to consume what they sell. The automotive industry has now responded to the trend. Rapper P. Diddy (Sean Combs) has come out with a set of custom rims called Sean John Wheels. The wheels were designed "specifically to reflect the sexy, sophisticated P. Diddy lifestyle."[3]

But what's cool today will soon change. Cool is always on the move.

Is cool free? You know the answer. No. In fact, chasing cool is very costly. It will always cost you more than you want to pay. The lure of cool is that not just anybody can afford it, so you pay more for whatever to gain some semblance of status and thereby weed out some of the poor riffraff, putting yourself closer to the top.

And for those of you, like me, who acknowledge you were never cool in school, don't think you are exempt from the temptation. You aren't. And I'm not just talking to young people here. This still applies to adults in many ways.

We can all pay the high cost of chasing cool. And I believe it's one of the most damaging things happening in our families today, especially in homes that are trying to follow Christ.

Chasing cool and chasing materialism seem to run together. And as always, the most harmed are always the young. Listen to two contemporary voices on this subject. Gary Ruskin writes about how advertising has taken our children down this dangerous road.

He says, "Advertising is a type of curriculum—the most persuasive in America today. . . . They teach that the solution to life's problems lies not in good values, hard work, or education, but in materialism and the purchasing of more and more things."[4]

I have three girls, aged 15, 7, and 3. I can tell you for certain that TV, radio, and print ads get stuck in their heads. All of them when they were very young would forsake the TV programming for the commercials. They would memorize the songs and want to buy the stuff and never even understand why. That's the job of an advertiser: To create a need and then fill it. Advertisers are great at enticing you to spend money you don't have on things you don't need. I mean, really, when was the last time you actually used your ThighMaster or Pocket Fisherman?

American family life shows that this pursuit of cool is a never ending cycle. Suburban parents line up to pay big dollars for private lessons to "you name the expert of whatever." They spend more time commuting to things than they do connecting with each other. And their kids end up being lifeless experts at self-indulgence, their lack of joy being evident by the time they spend acting bored. Never in the history of the world have children been given so many opportunities to please themselves. All of the family life is focused on them and their pursuits. There is no time for serving others outside the family and little time in there for God-worship at all. Families have substituted activity for love. In the United States we are busier and wealthier than ever before. But by no means are we getting happier. Psychologist David Myers writes:

> After four decades of rising affluence . . . are we happier than before? We are not. Since 1957, the number of Americans who say they are "very happy" has declined from 35 to 32 percent. Meanwhile, the divorce rate has doubled, the teen suicide rate has nearly tripled . . . and more people than ever (especially teens and young adults) are depressed. I call this soaring wealth and shrinking

spirit "the American paradox." More than ever, we have big houses and broken homes, high incomes and low morale . . . In an age of plenty, we feel spiritual hunger.[5]

I know that you may be thinking you gave up chasing cool a long time ago. But have you now, really? Let's reflect. Who do you spend your free time with? People you find that are behind the times and considered uncool? Do you generally hang out with people on a lower economic rung? Just a thought. Now think about what drives your purchases. Need or want? Our donations to Goodwill each year remind me how much of our clothing is really purchased based on what we need.

We all are victims of fashion to some degree, but it's another thing to be a fashion slave, isn't it? Did you buy that car because of the value or what it would say about you? What drives your career path and the job you will and will not take? Upward mobility or fulfilling God's calling? We all want to earn a living, but when does it cross the line into greed?

What about parenting? Are you more concerned about your child's social fulfillment or his or her spiritual life? It used to be that Christian parents would say in effect, "No matter what, I want my child to be a good student and a good citizen and to know Christ." Today's parents are obsessed by what others say is important.

They live a life captivated by the prayer "O God, don't let my kid be uncool. He [or she] may be unchurched, unmotivated, and unchristian, but don't let him [or her] be unpopular."

So since Jesus reserved His most poignant words for His people, I will try to do the same in this book. I am not trying to write a book of encouragement and deep comfort. You will already find the Christian bookstores lined with titles telling you how good you are. This book is written for a different purpose. It's a book that is aimed at shedding light by cutting through the layers of lies we are fed every day by a culture that's in the dark. I am writing so that you might just see this evil influence in your life and get off the treadmill of chasing cool. And if you do that, you will be encouraged and comforted deep in your soul. The solutions I set out are written primarily to those who are already convinced that following Christ is probably the best way to live. I am writing to those who believe that God's Word is true and provides the best picture of what the good life truly is. My hope is that you will read this book with an eye into your own soul. Don't let this be the book that so-and-so needs to read to help him or her. Let it help you too.

The god of cool is a real god. His followers are everywhere, in churches and out, chasing his image.

And if you chase him, you'll unknowingly waste your life. So let me give you a few answers I have found that really work in this alternative lifestyle that we call following Christ. I'm a slow learner, but when I do finally find something that works, I hold on like a pit bull. And the only thing that really works for me is Jesus—He's "it." So let's hear what He says to get us started on the right foot.

2

LADDERS AND BUGS

Seven Things That Cool Can Kill

In him was life, and that life was the light of men. The light shines in the darkness, but the darkness has not understood it (John 1:4-5).

I went to Lowe's the other day. I don't belong in Lowe's. They have dangerous things there. Things that could put an eye out and stuff. I mean, I took shop class in ninth grade and made a table for me and a stool for my mom. I still have the table, and my mom still has the stool. It's the same stool she has tried to return to me on numerous occasions since, citing that their dwelling is "too small" and that I probably needed it more than her. My mom is not very sentimental about my stuff. (But she does love me!)

I am not a master craftsman by any stretch, but I do know how to plug in power tools. But again, I don't belong in Lowe's. I guess one reason that I don't belong there is that I forget the little details. You know, the things that builders get all caught up in, like down to 1⁄16". You know the saying they use, "measure twice and cut once"? I hate that saying.

So I bought a ladder. When I worked in insurance, I had a ladder like this, the kind they advertise on TV that will telescope up and fold into a neat little package and can be programmed to make breakfast for you and all. My detail problem came into full view when I unfolded it and realized it was a lot shorter than I expected. I mean, it looked as though it could do the job folded up, but the unfolded version didn't add that much height. I had bought a 12' ladder for a 16' job. But you know guys and tools. My wife, Mindy, asked when I was taking it back. She likes taking things back and is much wiser in matters of finance than I. But there was no way I would be taking this thing back. The moment I ripped the package off, we became emotionally connected.

So I found something I could do with it—change the light bulbs on our front porch. Mindy had given up on me changing them a long time ago. I said, "Well, if I had a ladder, I'd do it." She rolled her eyes knowing that any good husband would borrow the neighbor's, but she let me off and let it go. Mindy does that a lot—lets me off the hook, I mean. God blessed me with a patient wife. Meanwhile, our front porch lights stayed out for more than a year. So now I had the ladder, the ladder and I were one, and the lights would now get changed. Adding the cost of the ladder, it totaled $104 to change those light bulbs. And it was worth every penny.

But there's more to this story. See, the light bulbs were inside a fixture mounted to the ceiling. And somehow the fixture had enough space in it for bugs of all kinds to fly in and buzz around the light. There were even some crafty spiders who had figured out where the bug party was going to be and put their webs up right in the middle of it. But it looked as if all the bugs were dead. I mean, they were piled an inch high and were stuck together in this big dead bug fabric of sorts. When I finally dumped them out, they all came out in a dried clump.

I had this intuitive thought that these bugs had missed something. They had come to this light bulb expecting something, but that something was never delivered, and it ended up being their final resting place rather than the big bug party that it appeared to be. They were drawn to the light by instinct. Bugs need light, I guess. And there were other bugs present, doing the same thing, but they all chose the wrong light. The sad thing is that now that the light bulb is shining again, many bugs are going to give their lives by chasing the substitute, and it's all my fault.

So why is it that bugs get fooled so easily? I mean, look at the fly. He's got about a million eyes. He's got to be able to see that there's something wrong with buzzing a light bulb, doesn't he? Flies truly are stupid. So what's our excuse? People in this country get a free education and have the truth available to them on the best way to live. People would never be as dumb as a multieyed housefly and choose the wrong light, would they? I mean, what's causing folks to choose a life that will ultimately be harmful both now and eternally?

Author Donald Miller believes there's something behind all of this, causing us to want the wrong things in life. "Here is the trick, and here is my point. Satan, who I believe exists as much as I believe Jesus exists, wants us to believe meaningless things for meaningless reasons."[1] Satan puts up a different light. And this deception causes people to follow it. And when they follow the wrong light, they end up in the dark. And when people are in the dark, they can't see. And when they can't see, they don't believe the right things, and all people who do wrong things do them mainly because they believe wrong things. Bad beliefs always lead to bad behavior. Not because people are stupid but because they are deceived, just like the bugs. Oh, and did I mention that Jesus said that people are a lot like sheep? Sheep don't think much either—they just put their heads down and graze wherever the other sheep are grazing, oblivious to the wolves around them.

The people I meet don't appear to be as stupid as flies or as silly as sheep. Most of them speak in full sentences, know how to brush their teeth before bedtime, and are able even to pass the most stringent of all human tests, the driver's license exam. I deal with geniuses mostly. But these same geniuses (OK, I'm in that group too) are the same ones who way too often choose the wrong light to follow in life. And as a pastor, I get to see the results when people tell me about all the skeletons in their closets.

But bad beliefs always lead to bad behavior. Miller writes, "Even our beliefs have become trend statements. We don't even believe things because we believe them anymore. We only believe things because they are cool things to believe."[2] Like now, among most 20-somethings, it's perceived to be cool to be a Democrat. In a decade the trend could reverse. Never mind what they may or not believe. It doesn't really matter what they believe, just that the right people believe it.

Here's the honest truth. It's sometimes hard to figure out which light is right. Jesus left earth and left it to people with skin on. And that's the whole problem associated with chasing cool, or anything for that matter, other than the true light—Jesus Christ. The apostle John tells us to walk in the light. But we have to choose the right light to walk in: *the* light. And it's the job of the Holy Spirit to direct us to this light. God wants the best for us and will show us how to walk in His marvelous light. But beware—if you choose the wrong light, there's a bug pile you might have to clean up.

Choosing the wrong light of cool could cost you—

1. Happiness. Part of the reason depression is on the rise is that nobody can measure up. All the people we look at very long are better than us somehow. If you're a pastor like me, you can begin to compare yourself to all the guys who are more clever, creative, and successful. If you start to work out and you look at muscle magazines, you get depressed. Maybe you felt good about your body image earlier that day, but one picture of Flex Wheeler did you in. Celebrity worship never provides the happiness it promises. If you look at the entertainment shows and magazines about the beautiful people, it can bring you down. Those people seem to have what we need, so we try to get in their business. Paparazzi keep us in the loop to let us know that the stars are just as imperfect as us. But even after we know the dirt about them, we don't feel happy. When you fly after the wrong light of cool, it will never make you happy. Here's why. Because you are choosing to direct your life after something you can't define. It's like the bugs who don't even know what light they are really supposed to fly after. So you wouldn't even know it if you were to get it. Chasing cool is like trying to nail Jell-O to a wall. It just doesn't work and will never make you happy.

2. Money. Since cool is a perception that constantly changes, you have to keep up with the purchases made by those perceived as cool. Tom Sine writes, "We have become a nation of unpaid walking billboards for branded products."[3] I am always amazed that people will pay $50.00 for the privilege of wearing something like Abercrombie on their chest. And, by the way, don't you feel a little sorry for Fitch? Fitch is like the modern underdog of the mall. Kind of like the sad story of Sears and Roebuck. I always felt sorry for Roebuck. He was on the sign, for goodness's sake. He had to be a good guy to hook up with Sears and all—but where is he today? (By the way, last week in our mall, Abercrombie had its own male topless model, live and in person. With his ripping six-pack abs and inviting smile, he was signing

T-shirts for adolescent giggling girls. Looks like a bug pile forming. Oh, and did I mention that their mothers brought them to this extravaganza of virtue?) Sheep are not smart.

I am definitely not immune to overspending for image. I remember purchasing our first house right out of college. We went for way more house than we could afford so that it would appear that we were on the rise—a couple with a load of cool. I remember sitting in this big, beautiful house with no furniture eating Ramen noodles every meal. We spent a lot of years with an empty big house and a great big house payment.

If you've ever purchased a new car, you remember fondly those first few days of enjoying all the extra options, that tight feel around the corners, and the famous new car smell. You tool around town looking in the mirrors, noticing everyone who is admiring your new car. You wash it every day to make sure the dirt doesn't grind in and mar the image of this new piece of you. But at some point you get a little paranoid. You start noticing the other "beaters" in the parking lots and end up parking way out all alone. Then you start worrying about hail damage, willow tree sap, or freak opossum damage to the undercarriage. Once you start worrying about your car, there's no end to the things that could go wrong, so you decide to install the car alarm that says, "Step back or I'll shoot." Instead of owning the car, it now owns you. In extreme cases a person may even wear the emblem on ball caps and T-shirts and display them as proudly as a grandparent with school pictures. In fact, when people ask for family photos, pictures of the car come out of the wallet first. OK, maybe this is a little over the top, but when you own stuff that owns you, anything can happen.

3. Time. You'll spend your time doing things that cool people tell you are important. I remember back in high school in Odessa, Texas. I was told that all the popular people cruised the strip. So my friend Allan and I did too. Allan had an illegal driver's license the state had issued him. It said he could drive without a parent, even though he was only 15. His dad figured the license was the law, and Allan got a car. (Allan really looked about 12 when he was 15.)

Finally we got to see what all the fuss was about. I mean, the kids at school made it seem like the best thing ever was to go cruising. So the first night out, I was thinking, "OK, did we miss the deal? This isn't *that* much fun." I mean, we would go up a mile, hit the mall, and then turn around in the parking lot, biceps flexing on the open window frame, yelling out a squeal if we saw any female wearing inappropriate clothing. But that was about it—for hours. So we would stop for a burrito (cruising and flexing and yelling burn calories, you know) and park in the mall lot and eat and talk about how much fun we were about to have when the cruising really got hot.

It didn't take me long to realize that being cool took too much time, and I just didn't care enough to drive around long enough to get it.

As an adult, chasing cool will keep you at work and keep you busy. Working long hours and complaining about it is the height of male cool.

If you have kids, they will have to be on the most competitive sports teams. Translated, that means you're going to pay a lot of money so that your less-than-competent coaching friend can yell at your kids a lot, all in the name of making them better athletes with a chance for a scholarship, beginning at age three. And all the while they will travel the country looking for other cool teams to play against when the ones in your own city run out of cool. I saw a bumper sticker that said "Jesus is coming soon—look busy." It's cool to look busy.

4. People. Chasing the wrong light of cool always requires that you leave behind any friends who may do damage to your cool. Uncool is catchy and must be avoided at all costs. When I was a kid, uncool was called the cooties. As a first grader I thought the cooties were head lice. I don't know how I made that connection but I remember learning the truth in second grade. I decided then that getting head lice would be better than having the cooties. So if you happened to like the kid who others said had cooties, then he or she had to go.

In junior high school we began the natural selection segregation process of placing people in the jocks, cheerleaders, nerds, geeks, brains, band people, and heads categories. You didn't hang out with the geeks, even if you happened to be one. (And everybody wanted to hang out with the cheerleaders, but nobody I knew got to.) Chasing cool will cost you people who may be the ones God wants you to hang out with.

5. Your reputation. Chasing cool could put you with a group of people who are perceived as cool but will make you guilty by association. For instance, it may make you buy clothes that are in style but indecent. Do you ever wonder who came up with the idea of hip huggers for young females that show their little tan tummies? You know who it was, don't you? It was every ninth grade boy in the world. Some of those boys grew up to be designers. (Even though some of them still may not like girls as much.)

I heard a study on the news last week that kids that are perceived as popular or cool are twice as likely to get into trouble with the law as the nerds. I'm not making this up—I promise.

6. Your family. For many grown-ups, immorality and fast living is seen as cool. I have heard from executives who travel a lot. These aren't Christian types, so they don't conceal what they are up to. They even brag to one another about their exploits and conquests while out on the road.

Parenting by cool is a suburban epidemic. Many parents bow to parent peer pressure and let their kids run wild rather than putting up healthy boundaries that save kids from drug addiction, premature sex, and other pressure that kids should not have to handle on their own. The result is kids who have never been told "no." (Then these same kids enter the real world very soon expecting a world without boundaries and are shocked when their employers say the very things their parents were afraid to say.) Thankfully, my mom was good at "no."

7. Your soul. Jesus said it best this way, "And how do you benefit if you gain the whole world but lose your own soul in the process? Is anything worth more than your soul?" (Matt. 16:26, NLT). That's a question for every cool chaser. I think it's the question they are asking in bug heaven. The smart bugs are probably saying, "And how did we benefit from chasing that light bulb? Didn't it just cost us our bug souls?" The light bulb fools the bugs, and a lot of things fool us too.

The enemy of our souls is literally the king of copies. He has never had an original thought in his head, but he can steal a good idea and try to copy it. He will try to lure us in with promises he can't back up, and history is littered with the lifeless and deceived. Chasing cool is always a detour that promises a shortcut but delivers a dead end. It's a light that promises illumination but delivers darkness.

The way out of the chase isn't one and done. There's no magic pill you can swallow that will make you immune to deception. No prayer you can recite to make you bulletproof. But you can begin the slow process of Spirit-induced change and learn to avoid some of the misguiding lights. And it's my hope that the rest of this book will offer some insight in refocusing your eyes on the one true Light. Look at what the good brother John said about this Light: "If we walk in the light, as he is in the light, we have fellowship with one another" (1 John 1:7).

John said there is a right light to walk in. Jesus is the right Light. And every good walk gets started after you take at least one step in a particular direction. Writing to his former congregation in Ephesus, the apostle Paul said, "You were once darkness, but now you are light in the Lord. Live as children of light" (Eph. 5:8). In other words, you used to buzz the wrong light, but you don't fly the same way anymore.

As my ninth grade marching band instructor would say, "It's time to step it up!"

3

WEATHERMEN DON'T HAVE TO BE RIGHT

The New Pursuit Starts in the Heart

Love the Lord your God with all your heart (Mark 12:30*a*).

Weather is a big deal in Oklahoma. We have a lot of tornadoes and tornadoes kill people, and we want people to tell us when and where the tornadoes may hit so we don't die. Weathermen are smart people in Oklahoma. Not like in Los Angeles, where all the guy has to learn to say is "sunny and 72, after the morning marine layer burns off." In L.A., you just have to have a really good serious look for the cameras and know your weather nomenclature really well when describing the weather back east. Oh, yeah, and the L.A. guy has to know how and why smog forms, but next to Oklahoma weathermen, L.A. weathermen are pansies. (No offense intended to any weathermen who may be reading this book. You are obviously smart.)

But you don't have to be right to be a weatherman in Oklahoma. They have this cool deal in weather predicting. It's called a "percentage chance." For example, if it may rain tomorrow, they say, "There's a 50 percent chance of rain"—which means it may rain, and it may not. Isn't that what every day is, really? I mean, every day you wake up, and it may rain or it may not rain. You don't have to go to weather school to know that, do you?

So getting back to the chance of rain deal, don't you wish you could have a job where you are wrong a lot and not get fired? Like your boss would come up to you and say, "Good job, son. You almost did it right. You lost our biggest account today because you were incompetent, but at least you tried." I think I'd like a job where it was OK to be wrong a lot.

But I'm a pastor, and being wrong is a really big deal in my line of work. People can get hurt if I'm wrong.

And they can get mad at you. If I tell them "chances are good that hell is just a city in California," I better be sure of that one. No percentage deal is available for hell talk. And if I say, "Jesus is the only way to eternal life," I'm saying that there's a 100 percent chance that there isn't another way. I guess I need to be pretty sure about that too. It seems that it would be easier to mention the percentage deal there for people—like a 95 percent chance that Jesus is the only way, to leave room for the skeptics and all, just so they could get in too. I think that's the way I might do it if it didn't matter if I was right all the time.

I do believe everything the Bible tells me about what Jesus said, though. I really believe it. So then I look at this conversation Jesus had with a guy. He was a smart guy who would have felt out of place as a weatherman in L.A. He wasn't into percentage chances on the truth either—he wanted to know what Jesus thought was a really big deal. Here's how the story goes:

> One of the teachers of the law came and heard them debating. Noticing that Jesus had given them a good answer, he asked him, "Of all the commandments, which is the most important?" "The most important one," answered Jesus, "is this: 'Hear, O Israel, the Lord our God, the Lord is one. Love the Lord your God with all your heart and with all your

soul and with all your mind and with all your strength'" *(Mark 12:28-30).*

I feel that after He said this Jesus gave the teacher a Clint Eastwood, Dirty Harry (with his squinty eyes closed and his teeth grinding together) look, saying, "Well, do you . . . punk? Do you really love the Lord like that?" This guy was trying to back Jesus into a corner, and Jesus wouldn't have any of it. He gave the teacher the 100 percent truth, and the teacher listened.

And this same story is for us today. If we came up to Jesus with skin on and asked Him this question tomorrow, His answer would be the same. So look at it closely. Jesus says, if you are a Christ follower, this heart thing isn't an optional command—it's an imperative.

Now in this verse the heart doesn't refer to the muscle that pumps blood through your body. It refers to what you desire most. For instance, my wife, Mindy, owns my heart. She owns my desire as far as women go. She's the only woman I would enjoy being stranded with on a deserted island. She's the sugar in my coffee and the honey on my bun. She makes life sweeter for sure. Part of our marriage vows say that she is the only one to get this kind of desire.

On Valentine's Day, the official holiday invented by greeting card companies, we have pictures of hearts everywhere. We send candy and flowers to the one we desire because the calendar says February 14. (I have long suspected that Mr. Valentine was not really into the holiday but was an ancient ancestor of the Hallmark family, perhaps.)

So what owns your heart? Take a minute to pause and ponder that fact. What owns my heart? Hmm. One way to tell what owns your heart is in your quiet times. What does your mind tell you that you need to be doing? When I first got married and didn't have kids, I have to admit that I had a divided heart in some areas. I loved God and Mindy, but I also loved fishing. In fact, I probably thought about fishing in most of my free mind time in those days. I would read *Bassin'* magazine, talk fishing on the phone, plan fishing trips, and most importantly spend many hours on the lake, in my float tube or a friend's boat, with my love at the time, fishing. You know what they say about boats, don't you? "It's better to have a friend with a boat than to own one yourself." I thought that was a pretty wise saying for a guy with no money after a big house payment, so I became a boat mooch. (After all, they also say that a boat is really just a hole in the water you pour money into.)

Now there isn't anything wrong with fishing. Fishing is the most biblical sport out there. I don't see Jesus hanging out with racquetball players or soccer players, but He spent most of His time with guys who share this passion of mine. Fishing is probably the official sport of Jesus when you get down to it.

So if Jesus had said that heart question to me, face-to-face that day, I think I would have cringed. If He would have given me the Clint Eastwood look and said, "Well, do you love Me with all your heart?" I know the answer. I would have said, "Not really." Now over time, I do believe I have learned to put this into practice in my own life and love God first, but it isn't easy. The reason it isn't easy is that I like to make me comfortable and I like to think about me first.

But here's the cool thing. Since I've made this commitment to God and told Him He has my heart, He has given me something new. He has fulfilled His promise and taken my "heart of stone" and made it a "heart of flesh" (Ezek. 11:19).

Since that time, the Holy Spirit keeps working on me like a sculptor on a stone, asking me to open myself up to become more like Christ. I've got a new heart but a lot of rough edges. Weathermen don't have rough edges, on account of great hair and makeup people.

I like the old story about the sculptor who was chiseling a block of granite to form a beautiful horse. A guy asked him how he did it. And he said simply, "I take the block of granite and chip away everything that doesn't look like a horse." God does that with us when we offer

Him our heart. We make the commitment to sit there while He chisels. We begin to open our inner lives and let God remove the junk that keeps us looking ugly and less than we could and should be. When we agree with God, and do remove the unnecessary dark areas from our life, a new picture of our best self slowly begins to unfold. Unfortunately, since we have been graced with a free will, we can always walk away from God's work on us and take a break. God will never force His image on us; He does so only with our total cooperation.

Theologians blame this self-first mentality on original sin. It makes sense to me. My three girls were all born with my disease of wanting their own way. One of the first words they learned was *mine!* If they don't like something, they whine and fuss until you get it for them. Have you heard the toddler's motto? "If I have it, it's mine. If you have it, it's mine. If I can see it, it's mine." Babies learn early on that "It's all about me."

Growing up, my brother Chris and I used to go to the carnivals passing through town, and we paid to go through what they called a fun house. One of the cool things about it was the way the floors and walls and ceilings slanted at different angles that were more severe than normal. And as you walked through the fun house, it would make you lean one way or another. This original sin thing in us is more like a lean, I think. We lean toward the easy thing, loving ourselves, and we lean away from loving God. Our heart is bent toward our own agenda and away from God's. It's just within us to want our own way.

For a second here, let me talk about the weather again. I like the Weather Channel, and I like trees.

In Oklahoma the wind blows all the time, especially in the western half of the state. The prevailing wind is out of the south most of the year. This gives the taller trees in western Oklahoma a slight lean to the north. They didn't do anything wrong to lean that way. They were forced into leaning by the conditions around them. They do their best to continue to reach up to the sun, but the wind is always pushing on them, trying to get them to lean north.

That's a little bit of how I think of our inborn selfish tendency. We entered a fallen world at birth and the wind of our nature and the winds of culture continue to blow. As we grow, we try to resist and reach upward, but it's always easier to go with the bent—almost as if straight up and down isn't natural anymore. And not only are our hearts bent, but our world is also bent like the floors of the fun house causing us to stumble and lean the wrong direction even when our intentions are right.

And then Jesus comes with this command, "Love the Lord your God with all your heart" (Mark 12:30), as if it may really be possible. This makes me think a lot about many of the Christian authors I read. They don't like this verse very much, or at least they don't like to talk about it with the same tone as Jesus. I don't picture them looking like Clint Eastwood when they talk about this one, more like Mister Rogers. (I do think Fred was cool, though.) Many Christian writers seem to treat having a loving heart more like an impossible option than a direct command. But I'm going with Jesus on this one. If He says it's possible, He's the Creator of the universe. He invented salt.

Think about this. Things always start in the heart, don't they? Think about your last big impulsive purchase. Like my ladder, for instance. What motivated me to buy that thing anyway? Well, it was a desire that grew into reality. I wanted to fix something. My want affected my behavior.

A few years back, my heart's desire was to get in shape at home. So I purchased the stair-stepper, which soon became more junk on the back porch and last month got smashed in the trash truck. My desire, or heart, drove me to make a soon-to-be wasteful purchase. I use these examples not to say that purchasing exercise equipment or even ladders is evil. The intent was honorable. But it points to how our desires drive our actions.

So do you desire God deep down? Do you think about Him when there's nothing going on? Is your heart tuned to His voice? If you are going to love God with all your heart, you must begin to desire what God desires. And here's some disconcerting news: He's not at all concerned about your cool status. He cares a whole lot more about your character than your cool.

Back in the Old Testament, the Israelites lost a generation who loved God and God's leader Joshua. Maybe your parents love Jesus, but you aren't that fired up. If that's you, your relationship with God needs to start fresh, right now. Or you will be trapped just like thousands before you. Look back at what those Israelites did. "They abandoned the LORD, the God of their ancestors" (Judg. 2:12, NLT). Every generation has a choice, and so do you.

The apostle Paul wrote this to the Christ followers at Colosse, "Since, then, you have been raised with Christ, set your hearts on things above, where Christ is seated at the right hand of God" (Col. 3:1).

Now I'm not sure what it means to set my heart, but I think it's a little like when you realize the person you like and love will eventually be the person you are going to marry. When I set my heart on Mindy, I started making plans. I started bringing up the possibility for marriage and examined her face for nervous twitching or any other latent sign of disinterest or disgust. They didn't appear. The signs suggested I was on the right track. I had set my heart on Mindy, and she seemed to feel the same way.

So to continue in my quest for my Lady Guinevere, I did what all men do. I started watching for diamond ring sales. And when the time was right, just as God had planned it, I'm sure, Treasures Inc. had a 75 percent off sale on wedding sets. God had spoken. It was time to make the move. After a conversation with my father-in-law that could have been written by Rod Serling for *The Twilight Zone,* I got the OK, and I was going to make the move. (While I was asking Dillard for his daughter's hand, he looked like Clint Eastwood but never looked at me while we sat at the kitchen table, and he scraped the cheese and sauce off his pizza and spread peanut butter on it!)

I was in college at the time and was working full time at a hotel. I had enough money to pay for the ring but not a fancy engagement dinner. So I did what any romantic would do. I took Mindy to Taco Bueno. I had this plan that I would ask her in the parking lot to get something out of the glove box, and when she opened it, she would see the ring staring back at her. Well, the plan wasn't foolproof. The glove box opened prematurely, and I nervously slammed it, and she knew something was up. But I still went through the little charade, and she said yes when I asked her, and she promised she would give me her heart as well. And thankfully, we have been married now for 21 years with things improving all the time.

So when I set my heart on things above, it's like making a promise that from now on I am going to think about and try to please the One who has my heart. If you really want to live the blessed life, your heart must be with God. There's no better way to live the good life.

See—when you chase cool, you are consumed by what others think about you. The court of public opinion is the most important to the cool chaser. Image becomes everything. But when you chase Christ, I mean really give Him your heart, only His opinion counts.

But don't let me tell you it's easy. It isn't. Ask any married couple if staying married is easy. Relationships are hard, so focus is critical. It's easy to forget what got you together in the first place. I see it happen all the time when folks forget and choose divorce.

In the Psalms, King David understood what it took to stay focused like this. "Teach me your way, O Lord, and I will walk in your truth; give me an undivided heart, that I may fear your name" (Ps. 86:11).

Look at those words: *undivided heart.* David was just a man like all of us men. He had a lot of desires racing his way. The Bible tells us he was nice-looking, charismatic, gifted in music, physically strong, a gifted leader, and a fearless man of faith. And God called him "a man after my own heart" (Acts 13:22).

So have you committed your heart to Jesus, really? And have you allowed Him to begin to chip away the rough edges that keep you from loving Him as you should?

The temptation will always be to give our heart away to something else, to chase something that doesn't really matter. David knew he needed God's help in the heart department. And so do we.

So what are the atmospheric conditions in your relationship with God? Do you truly love God with all your heart or are things a little foggy? Are you pursuing your relationship with Him above everything else, or are you letting the storms of choice overcome your heart? If you ever want to quit wasting your life chasing cool, your heart must change first.

4

MIND TRACKS

Keeping Your Mind Focused When You Try to Stay Out of Old Mental Ruts

Your workmanship is marvelous—and how well I know it (Ps. 139:14*b*, NLT).

I really love being outdoors in the daylight. I love hiking up mountains, getting my hands dirty, and sweating, even with sweat bees swirling over my head. I love the clear scents of pine and cedar wafting through the dry mountain air. But I don't love sleeping outside in sleeping bags or where there may be bears. Rather, I love that when I get done with my hike, I'll get back in my air-conditioned car stocked with plenty of Disani-brand water. In summary, I like the outdoors, but I don't want to live there. I learned that on my first and only camping trip to Estes Park, Colorado. (Details of which will be forever undisclosed.)

From my air-conditioned comfort I was watching a remake of *Little House on the Prairie* the other night. With all the less-than-desirable stuff on TV, I figured it was a family opportunity. (All but my oldest tuned out before the first 30 minutes were over.) This "Little House" was a lot grittier and tried to be a little more realistic in its portrayal of the conditions faced by our westward-moving settlers in the 1800s than the Michael Landon version of my childhood. I sat on my comfy couch, eating apple dippers, in awe of what it must have been like to travel hundreds of miles by covered wagon. Those people were tough: tough like the bottom of leather shoes. Tough like beef jerky without the plastic resealable bag. I mean they had this big idea in mind, getting out west with the free land and all, and they weren't going to let anything stop them. Tough, outdoorsy people.

One of the scenes in the movie had the family trekking through the unpaved woodlands of Iowa. It's weird to think that they had never even seen or envisioned a four-lane road or traffic light. Car travel probably would have seemed like a sissy way to go for these folk anyway. And the octagonal stop sign would be decades away. I began to ponder and dream of what life would have been like without traffic and squealing tires, without engine noise and road rage. I started envisioning a log cabin by a stream with no windows. I heard the cricket sounds and whippoorwills replacing idling cars. I thought of the beauty of living at one with the land. This has always been my dream, I guess. That one day I could be a modern Jeremiah Johnson, big beard and all, where the bears and I would talk and arm wrestle and just hang out admiring our togetherness.

And then in my mind I walked over to my refrigerator to open a cold drink. But I had to stop and remember that in this wilderness there would be no electricity and no fridge. There weren't any windows in my little woodsy hideaway, and I got itchy because mosquitoes love the wilderness and flowing streams and people like me. And before lying down on my bed that rested on a dirt floor, I remembered ticks. I hate ticks. But ticks aren't that picky. They like things with blood in them—things like me. And ticks like the woods because animals live there, like deer and elk, who don't have fingers and who can't pull them off. And ticks could hide on the wall of a log cabin house and eat me for breakfast before I even knew what hit me, along with chiggers. (I know that ticks came as a result of Adam and Eve's sin somehow.) And since my floor would be dirt, don't get me started on all the boring animals I saw poking their heads up in my direction. So all of a sudden I liked the future, even with crabby drivers. I guess I'm sort of outdoorsy with a bent toward civilization.

So the Ingallses were in this schooner, plowing through the woods on the path that seemed to be there, and then they started to bog down. The tracks on the trail were passing through an area of land that didn't drain very well. And they got stuck. Getting stuck in the mud is never a good thing for a covered wagon—because not only do the wheels get stuck but so do the horses. And when the horses get stuck, it's time to get help or start building a house. You aren't going anywhere anytime soon.

The truth is that our mind has tracks just like a wagon traveling on a dirt path. The longer you travel the road of life, the deeper the ruts become. This is good when you're on a good road leading to a good place in life. But it's really bad when the rut you run in continues to lead you into the boggy places and you can't seem to figure out how to quit going down that road.

You know that going there will cause pain, but programming just seems to take over.

Married couples have these mind tracks that can be good and bad. They get along great until it comes to a certain issue, and then they just bog down. Their mind tracks led them here. And instead of taking the high ground around a constant problem, and cutting a new trail, they can resort to put-downs and historical failures and they never make it out of their rut. Probably the biggest cause of marriage failure is a failure to make new mind tracks.

In the last chapter I talked about giving your heart to God. That's a pretty hard deal indeed. But focusing your mind isn't that easy either. And when it comes to *cool,* most people chase *cool* because that's what they're told to do—not purposely rejecting God, just following the ruts of generations past. Our example, the Israelites, simply forgot all that God had done, and that thinking got them into this rut of idolatry. The apostle Paul cautioned one of his churches that if you want to learn the way to stay out of the ruts and boggy conditions, you must find a way to get to the high ground. He said, "Set your minds on things above, not on earthly things" (Col. 3:2). But how do you really set your minds on things above?

In the Old Testament David knew how to do it. He

was the king of Israel and the king of setting his mind above the unhealthy mind tracks of others. I'll talk more about him in a minute.

The other day I woke up, and I noticed the palm of my hand. I stopped as I considered the pattern of the waves of my handprint. I marveled at the intricate level of detail on my hands. Then I remembered that each fingerprint makes me different from everybody in the world. It blows me away to realize that nobody has the same pattern. I thought about the intro to the popular TV show *CSI: Crime Scene Investigators.* They do a lot with fingerprints and other clues to investigate murders. And during the intro they play the famous old song by The Who aptly titled "Who Are You?" Here's the deal—I can get out of the mind tracks that will harm me if somebody will tell me how. If I want to know who I am, the fingerprint will identify me. But the fingerprint doesn't tell anybody who I really am.

David knew that the key to his life was not in what he did but in who he was. In one of my all-time favorite Bible chapters, He writes in a rather high-minded way about the wonder of his own existence.

> You made all the delicate, inner parts of my body and knit me together in my mother's womb. Thank you for making me so wonderfully complex! Your workmanship is marvelous—and how well I

know it. You watched me as I was being formed in utter seclusion, as I was woven together in the dark of the womb. You saw me before I was born. Every day of my life was recorded in your book. Every moment was laid out before a single day had passed *(Ps. 139:13-16, NLT).*

One of the ways to stay out of bad mind tracks is to consider how important you are to God and understand that He loves you more than you can comprehend. In these verses I know that David was asking the big question in life. And really, the biggest question in the universe is made up of two words that all of us ask at different times in our life. We all ask it: Why me? Why am I here? What should I do? Where do I go?

I understand that God knows all of that. I really believe He knows that stuff, but I struggle here. There are days when all of us wonder who we are, why we are, and where we should go. For Christian people, I think this is a good thing. It keeps us focused on things above. Because most of the people you work with, golf with, or hang out with who are not believers don't spend a lot of time asking the big questions in life. They just don't spend as much time looking inward. They don't ask that question. Most just play follow-the-leader.

I think that's what keeps people in the rut of chasing cool. It seems to be the path that everybody takes because everybody else is taking it. We seem to be able to ignore the failure and emptiness we see all around us and think that it won't affect us. I heard an elderly evangelist say that the reason for our bad behavior was "stinkin' thinkin'." Stinkin' thinkin' is easy to see in others but harder to detect in ourselves.

David was able to steer clear of the rut of idolatry, and those verses give me great insight into setting my mind above. So let me remind you of a few things you have probably heard but need to ponder on a weekly basis.

God knows who I am, He knows what I am made of, and He has a plan for my life.

1. God knows who I am: "Thank you for making me so wonderfully complex! Your workmanship is marvelous—and how well I know it" (Ps. 139:14, NLT).

When I stared at my hand and noticed the prints, I looked at other parts of my body. My footprint is unique as well. Of the 6.6 billion people in the world, nobody wears a shoe or a mitten just like me. I look at my hand and hear this scripture ringing in my head. God's workmanship is marvelous. Even down to my left pinky finger that was broken at the last joint and grew back at a weird angle.

But sometimes we don't know who we are. When my daughter Hope was 17 months old, she once walked up to my office and stopped when she saw some men inside that she did not know.

She had been to my office before, but the men inside looked imposing for some reason. So she did what anybody would do. She lifted up her shirt until she could find her bellybutton.

It was a funny scene. It seemed as though she was thinking, *Hey, as long as my bellybutton is still in the place where I left it, I'm going to be OK.* She was secure in knowing she was still in the right place and that she was still who she thought she was. Hope needed to know she was in the right skin.

OK, maybe that's a stretch, but it's still a cute story and a reminder that all of us struggle with how we're made and who we are. I take great comfort in the fact that God knows me inside and out and still thinks I am worthy of spending time with. And I'm OK with God having all the inside information on me. He knows all my dirt. I know He won't tell anybody about all my mistakes. I know He won't gossip about my secret thoughts. I know He'll accept me because He knows everything, top to bottom, good and bad, and the Bible says He still loves me. "Before a word is on my tongue you know it completely, O LORD" (Ps. 139:4). God knows what I am thinking and what I am about to say. I wish He wouldn't always give me that freedom. My words have the tendency to be erratic and not always consistent with my confession of Christ.

A few years back, I was pitching in slow-pitch softball. I love sports, and I like to win in sports. These are my mind tracks, and the ruts run deep. So the umpire behind the plate started not liking me—at least that's how I saw it. I don't know why. I had to assume it was because of his fallen nature and his hatred of Christians—I mean, wouldn't you think that? OK, I now know that that was not a smart leap of intellect, but under the intense pressure of slow-pitch softball, what else could I conclude? So here was this obvious Christian-hater disagreeing with my idea of the perfect pitch. I walked a few people in a row on what I would call perfect strikes, and I let him know both verbally and nonverbally of my displeasure. He wasn't moved to see it my way. In fact, things got a little worse after that.

This obviously bigoted Christian-hater seemed to take it up a notch. My critique of his umpire worthiness seemed to have the opposite effect of what I had desired. And as you can imagine, things kind of escalated. He clearly now had it in for us, thanks to me. So another bad, evil call was made, and I responded with the righteous cry of "That's ridiculous. You're not smart." (OK, that was the gist, not the words in that order.) As soon as my comments flew out of my mouth, one of my parishioners—did I mention this was a church league? —let fly a single word. "Spiritual!" she said, as in "You're not acting like our shepherd but like a whacked-out sheep." God could have stopped those words, but He didn't. He knew them, and He knew they were coming, and He still let me be a pastor who would on occasion speak for Him. This is why I would be a very different god. I wouldn't let people like me speak for me. God loves me even though I don't always say nice things.

The apostle John said it this way: "How great is the love the Father has lavished on us, that we should be called children of God!" (1 John 3:1). I like that word *lavished. Lavished* means "went over the top, bordering on too much." He lavishes love on mouthy pastors and Christian-hating umpires in the church league. God isn't picky like us.

And since God knows who you are, it's always good to devote a mind track to Him. In fact, it's even good to worship God for who you are. David said it like this, "I praise you because I am fearfully and wonderfully made" (Ps. 139:14).

Have you praised God for you lately? I know that sounds self-centered, but you really should. Here's why. He made only one version of you. I know that sounds corny and what we tell little kids so they don't feel bad after nobody would play with them on the playground, but we need to remember it as adults.

I used to collect coins. Coin collectors look for coins that are rare. I saw one on the Internet that was date-stamped with '99 when it should have been stamped '98. When the coin makers saw the mistake, they started over, but a few of these made it into circulation. Once collectors found out about it, these coins soon became really valuable. Scarcity made them valuable.

Valuable art is valuable because there's only one original. Real art collectors don't value copies, no matter how good. They value the one and only piece of art that was copied.

Another neat thing about coin collecting is that coins with flaws and idiosyncrasies are worth the most money. They're valuable because they're messed up, and there aren't very many like them.

We understand that one-of-a-kinds are priceless in art and literature. But there are more important things like "other people" we need to throw in that mix. I thought about the way God values uniqueness and how we value conformity. So why don't we value what God values in other people? Why are we so hard on each other to line up and be like everybody else?

It seems we value conformity over individuality when it comes to people. Everybody has to dress alike, talk alike, and value the same things, or they're outcasts.

You see this all the time, usually beginning in junior high school and continuing throughout life. The people who are unique are called names like "geek" or "nerd," while the people who conform most often are usually called "normal" or "popular." Usually after high school we call the unique ones "boss."

Conformity is a big deal and a deep rut. But, really, you don't have to conform to anybody's model of success. You *are* special. So what if people have denied your abilities or made fun of how you look? They didn't make you—God did. You need to worship the God who made you as you are. He took the mold that He used for you, and He broke it. You are valuable for that fact alone. God didn't copy you—you are it. You bear God's glory in a way that nobody else could. If you were a coin, and the coin maker stamped an original and then threw away the mold, you would be worth millions. The *Mona Lisa* is a masterpiece, and Mona isn't even that pretty. But she's one of a kind. The value is found in the subtlety of the way da Vinci made her smile. It looks like a little smirk.

God knows who you are, so worship Him. You are fearfully and wonderfully made.

2. God knows what I am made of: "You watched me as I was being formed in utter seclusion, as I was woven together in the dark of the womb" (Ps. 139:15, NLT).

It doesn't surprise God that you haven't won any money playing pro baseball. It doesn't surprise Him that you haven't won any beauty contests or a spelling bee or that you work better with your hands than you do listening to a lecture.

God knows what you and I are made of, and it doesn't surprise Him—but other people don't know what we are made of. And there's the problem. If we don't live our life fulfilling what God made us to be, we will always run after what others think we should be.

Other people tell us we should get a job paying a lot of money. You're more valuable if you're wealthy, they say. So we chase after their idea of what's best for us. Other people say you must climb the ladder to be a success—only the executives are really important. So you do as I did and try to pursue a position, and it makes you sick. We will always live our lives in desperation, in deep mud, trying to find what other people tell us we should be, if we miss what God made us to be.

God knows what you are made of. And He knows who you are. Since that is true, your lifelong challenge is to trust the God who knows what you are. He made you. All He wants is your love and trust. I would much rather trust God with my life, because He has insight that I don't. He knows the future.

The apostle James said it this way: "Now listen, you who say, 'Today or tomorrow we will go to this or that city, spend a year there, carry on business and make money.' Why, you do not even know what will happen tomorrow. What is your life? You are a mist that appears for a little while and then vanishes" (James 4:13-14).

God knows you are a mist that stays on this earth for only a little while. So don't tell God what you're going to do with your life and that you know best. You don't know the future any more than Brandini the magnificent. God knows what you are made of and what your tomorrow will look like.

In my own life, trusting God with my future is a give-and-take kind of deal. There are days when it's easy and days when it's not. I can wake up and tell God, "I'll do whatever You want. I know You love me and You know the future." But, then, in the middle of the same day I can ignore God's promptings and do what pleases me in that moment. Sometimes trusting God seems like a dance and I'm a horrible dancer. Two steps forward, two steps back. I feel that I am getting it right, but then I flop back into old steps that are unhealthy.

If we could see it from God's perspective, I think our dance of trust would look more like this: I am a part of His Church—His Bride. He takes my assent to His leading as authority to lead the dance. He hears the music better than me. He is able to stay on beat when I get tired, and He gets things to flow together. He lets me rest when I am exhausted, He doesn't let me go when I take a dip, and He keeps me headed on the right path when the music grows faint. "You chart the path ahead of me and tell me where to stop and rest. Every moment you know where I am" (Ps. 139:3, NLT).

I was raised with the thinking that God was just waiting on me to mess up and then drop me as His dance partner. But now I know that it's His dance, and I am there to bring Him glory. He thinks I am a good partner. So even with my mistakes and missteps, God is hanging on to me and pulling me close. This dance isn't over. In fact, it won't ever be over and will go on through eternity.

God knows I'm not a good dancer. But He knows I am letting Him lead. It's the only way He knows how to dance. You can trust Him with your life, your career, your family, and your future. He loves you the way you are because He made you the way you are.

3. God knows the plan for my life: "You saw me before I was born. Every day of my life was recorded in your book. Every moment was laid out before a single day had passed" (v. 16, NLT).

I have three girls: Jessica, Kelsey, and Hope. Before all three were born, we got to peer into the womb, via ultrasound, and see what God was making. We were able to see our kids before they were born. We studied their features and their movements. In Jessica's picture, we were able to see a perfect outline of her face and cute little nose at five months from conception. She looked exactly the same after she was born. We saw her before she was born. But that's about all we knew.

We didn't know her hair color, eye color, or disposition. We didn't know the name of her kindergarten teacher or the kind of food she would like. We didn't know if she would excel at school or have problems. We had no idea if she possessed any genetic problems that would lead to pain.

We still don't know if or who she will marry, where she will live as an adult, or what she will do for a career. We're good parents, but really we don't know much about what matters when it comes to our daughters. We can look at their pasts really well. We can see their lives unfold on videotape, but we don't have a camera into the future. God does. He knows every moment.

Now this does freak me out a little. I wish God would use this knowledge to step into my life more often and keep me out of the ruts. I wish He would do what I would do for my daughters if they were headed for trouble and save me first. Since He has a plan, shouldn't He do a better job making it happen?

Then I thought of teaching Jessica to ride a bike. I foreknew that when I took the training wheels off, she would fall down while riding. Everybody falls a lot at first. And then I thought about how God teaches me by allowing me to travel through some of my deepest ruts. He knows the ruts are coming and doesn't intervene. They're the same ruts I encountered last week—the same ruts I got severely bogged down in. But I'm learning that He allows me to experience the pain of failure to learn the joy of growth. See—God's plan for your life is not necessarily a career path. He may have a best fit for you, but He may have many career options.

Too many people get bound up thinking they need a certain career to follow God's plan. Here's the truth you need to know about your future. If you follow God, He will take you down the right path to the right job, at the right pace, with the right company. Enjoy the dance and let Him lead. He knows the way ahead, He knows why He made you and who you are, and He knows when the music will change from a joyful melody to a mournful dirge.

I was doing fine while working at the insurance company and was pretty happy there for the most part. But in my 30s a new season approached. The music was changing and the dance was about to transform. I followed God all those years in secular work, but He led me down another path. The dance continues and I still stink at dancing, but I'm learning not to step on the toes of the One who knows how to lead.

5

RANGER STATION

Staying Alert to the Cool Traps on the Horizon

You are the light of the world—Jesus (Matt. 5:14).

At age four I wanted to be a park ranger. I think it was the hats. Park rangers wear the coolest hats. Maybe it was the episodes of my favourite cartoon *Yogi Bear.* Yogi was pals with the ranger. I thought that was cool.

In national forests they have these tall towers where the rangers can look at their forest and see the possibility of fire. Fire is not good to a national forest. Well, that's not totally true. There are some fires that are good. Forestry people call these controlled burns—the idea being that if you start small fires in controlled areas, you can burn the underbrush but not the big trees. Fires that get out of control are fueled by too much underbrush. So every once in a while, some fire is good for a forest to weed out the potential for future devastation.

Life has good fire and bad fire. Bad fire is what gets me in trouble, and good fire has kept me from landing back in the trap of cool. Let me give you some of my personal history and a talk on fire. I promise it has a point.

A Heated Invitation

I had just turned 23, was married to my beautiful wife, Mindy, and had graduated from college with a degree in management. I had no problem with feeling qualified to manage. My sheepskin said I owned a bachelor's degree in it. *It must be something I am good at by now with all that great schooling behind me,* I thought. I had already been an assistant manager at a local motel during college. This management thing was a snap. "Just get a degree and give orders," I figured.

But as I soon learned, my degree brought few invitations to step in to the role as "the boss." I scanned the paper for management jobs and found little help. Finally I saw something that caught my eye. I think it said something like "entry level managers needed." I thought, *Hey, that's me. I am Supermanager.*

After showing up for the interview, I found out the job was really a financial services position, the idea being that I would offer financial planning to individuals with money who would pay me to spend their money for them—mostly on life insurance. The boss even said I could become a stockbroker someday. I knew less about the market than I did about life insurance, but I equated stockbroker with rich guy and instantly said, "I have always dreamed about doing that one day." This was true, but I also failed to include that it was one of about 1,000 *other* dreams that went through my gray matter—the main dream always ending in me being rich. So, as God would allow, the boss saw something in me that I wasn't really sure was there at all. I do believe the dream comment pushed me over the top. So I was hired with a six-month guaranteed salary: no production required. Thank God.

I soon learned that the financial services industry

was a tough racket. My main job was not stockbroking—it was life insurance sales. And as a 23-year-old with no money, no family or friends with money, no experience, and a boatload of debt while driving my dad's old car, I didn't strike up any quick relationships with fat cats who could line my wallet with all of their hard-earned *cha-ching*. In fact, I didn't really know many people who needed life insurance. Most of my friends were single and still being supported by their parents. I mean, really, young singles don't need life insurance in the first place. But this was my market, and away I went.

As you might guess, it didn't take long to call on everybody I had ever known as a friend. Then I called the friends of my closest relatives. Most were less than receptive, though a few did take me up on the idea. I think I sold a grand total of eight policies in six months—and three of those were sold to family (including one to me!). After my six-month guarantee, I was done. I knew my future must lie somewhere else. After all, that wasn't a real management job, and I am still a manager. And the bigger problem was that I didn't have any drive to sell the product. I knew deep down that the people I was talking to didn't really need what I was selling.

I still pursued the American dream as I understood it. The dream as I saw it went something like this: Go to college, and then find a job where you work as few hours as possible for the most money possible. Find your break-even point where the hours don't kill you and you can spend what you want, and live there.

Following my failed sales experience, I spent three years in credit and another eight in the insurance claims environment. Thankfully, neither of these were commission sales positions. In these jobs, the idea was again to work hard to climb the ladder to make more money to gain more power to make more money. All the while you must take some classes, make sure you stand out among your peers, and never tell the company you won't move when they ask, work late when they tell you to, or change jobs even if it's a bad fit.

I just became a good corporate soldier doing my duty. And in both positions I did quite well, promoting ahead of most of my peers. I was finally on the management fast-track. But something was still missing. I knew my job filled a need in the overall economy. I even finally comprehended why it takes years to learn how to manage, and I learned to respect those leaders that made me want to work harder. What was wrong?

From my earliest years I had been a Christian, raised in a pastor's home. And as an adult, I taught Sunday School every week and loved it. I even knew I could be a great Christian witness at work. All my buddies knew I loved Jesus and had gotten at least one invitation to my church. I was aware that I could live my faith in the workforce, but I needed something more.

More came in October 1997, when my life made its most dramatic shift. I heard the call by Coach Bill McCartney, the founder of Promise Keepers, to bring 1 million men to the Mall at Washington, D.C. When he talked about all those men praying for a nation and worshiping God Almighty, I knew I had to be there. So I made plans to meet my brother and his sons and drive up with them.

As preparation, I prayed and fasted for three days, which was a record for me. I thought, *Wow! Won't it be neat to see what God will do with that much prayer power coming together all at once, united in place and purpose.* I thought of all the Old Testament gatherings of Israel when a prophet or a king would address all of God's people. I envisioned the miraculous intervention of God moving to heal our nation. I just knew something great was going to happen. I just wasn't ready for what God had in store for me.

See, what God did for me that day has affected every day since. Here I thought He was going to change the nation, and what He wanted to do was to change me and through me bring change to the area of the world I lived in. In one moment, God filled me with a passion that was always in me—I just hadn't seen it.

One of the speakers at that event, Pastor Ronnie Floyd, said these words, "Some of you men are going to leave here today and go into full-time pastoral ministry." As he said that, I literally felt what seemed like arrows hitting me in the chest. I knew the hand and fire of God were thumping me like my football coach used to do when he put me in the game. God was sending me into the game in a new way. I bent over and wept about as hard as I could. I couldn't sit down because we were so packed together in the crowd, so I just stood there on holy ground contemplating just what this message would mean to me and my family. I knew everything would change, and that change was being fueled by an uncontainable passion to fulfill God's vision for my life.

I will tell you more about the rest of that story a little later. But this book is not about my life story or anything like that. This book is about what presses the button in a human soul that brings about the kind of soul change that is so desperately needed. I meet so many Christian people who struggle with depression and who feel they may have missed their life's purpose. They are rudderless ships with no direction or strength to change. They are like cars running on empty, miles from a gas station. They are good people but lack the strength to change. What's missing? And why does our culture keep driving all of us on this same boat to nowhere?

Let's back up a few years. In 1963 I was born into an age of passion. Being on the latter edge of the baby boom generation and more comfortable now as a buster, I have had the privilege of seeing the world really move. The 1960s and 1970s for most people were a time of marked, rapid social metamorphosis. Among the young, fashion styles of the day were an outer sign of these inner changes. Wacky bell-bottoms and tie-dyed fabric replaced the straight lines and simple colors of the past. Hairstyles for men went from short and neat to shaggy and long, while girls' skirts went from conservatively covering to barely there.

Political passions ran high as well. The Vietnam War was raging, and the new phenomenon of televised war coverage broadcast the brutal images for all to see. Now casualties of war were seen as real people, not just as numbers, and this enraged the masses. The pain of war was no longer a mystical, unseen element "over there." Suddenly, the "over there" came to our living rooms—and it just didn't seem to be right. Young men were dying for an uncertain goal in an unknown land. War was tearing the land apart and not many people understood why they were fighting in the first place.

(Even as I write, our nation is engaged in a war on terrorism. Over 100,000 soldiers are now in Iraq with no clear end in sight. Sadly, in some ways history seems to be repeating itself.)

Students were ignited by the pictures of their dying friends and schoolmates to the point of demonstrating against their own government. In protest, there were marches and mail campaigns, sit-ins and love-ins. Peace signs were worn around the neck, put on bumper stickers, and flashed by Richard Nixon. It was definitely an age of passion.

This passion also was seen in a new style of music. The transformation went from familiar chords, harmonies, and melodies of the 1950s to the loud and carnivorous growl of the electric guitar and the chest-thumping beat of rock-and-roll music. The beautiful crooner of days past was replaced by the angry voice of the antiestablishment. It was music with a passion to give up the sound of the past and show the world that the youth culture was a force of change to be reckoned with.

Combined with the music was the thread of radically open sexuality. Sensuality and sex outside of marriage were no longer taboo. It was the age of free love and doing whatever feels good. With the heightened focus on sharpening the senses, many other social mores failed and the drug culture was there to receive new victims. Marijuana and LSD gained widespread use and acceptance as an illegal, yet easily attainable alternative or additive to alcohol consumption. I entered the world in an age of life-changing passion.

Now enough has been written about the positive and negative effects of that era. I'm not here to break that ground again. Historians and others have weighed in on that. But I believe that the 1960s, as much as any other era in American history, illustrates the power that must undergird any radical change.

So here's my question: What was it that ignited the fires of change? Now, I'm not talking about what cause people were fighting for. The causes were many and diverse. What I am asking is this: once their cause was named, once the fight was chosen, what made these changes sweep the land like a wildfire? What is the one thing that is most needed for radical social and spiritual change to take place?

And since this is a Christian book, what is the one thing most needed by a majority of mature Christ followers? What is the one thing that is most often missing in a majority of American congregations? What was the thing I lacked while selling life insurance? What is the one thing so desperately missing from our culture that it stands out like a sore thumb when it's seen?

The answer, I believe, can be summed up in the one word I keep coming back to: *passion.*

Passion was the driving force behind the changes of the 1960s. Misguided though they may have been, none of those changes mentioned earlier would have happened in the vacuum of apathy and political correctness that we see so much today. Passion is a catalyst.

Passion is also needed before any other change in life can take place—a passion to right a wrong or meet a need that is unmet. Passion is needed before any Christ follower can make the changes that will ultimately lead to the spiritual growth that God dreams of for him or her. Passion is the one thing that can change a self-centered pew potato (like I used to be) into a mighty warrior for God. When rightly directed, passion can also lead to the kind of great awakening our culture needs to see so desperately. But passion is in short supply. And sadly, passion is the one thing that has died in so many American churches.

Passionless people sit in their pews week after week and go through the motions of spirituality. If you accused them of a lack of passion, they would quickly point to their attendance record in refutation. They come to worship God as if they are working in a factory. They get their bulletin from the usher and wave it at God like a holy time card. "See, God, I'm a good person,

I came to church today. See, other church people, I'm here, so I'm holy—*so stay off my back!*" They may sing a song and hear a good word, but they go home and there is no change. Their time with God is now perfunctory, not inflammatory. The fire that once burned within has gone from a flicker to a smolder. It has lost its meaning. The flame is gone.

Passion on Trial

It's easy to see why passion is very rare in our culture today. If you stand for something these days, get ready to take some shots. If you stand out and stand up, there are plenty of people around who are waiting to knock you down.

During the 2004 Democratic primaries, Vermont Governor Howard Dean learned this lesson the hard way. Following early losses on the opening night of the Iowa caucuses and New Hampshire primary, Dean gave a speech to rally his troop of supporters. During this speech, he got fired up and began to "preach instead of teach," if you know what I mean. And at the end of his passionate plea, he let out this growling, yelling sound that was more like a James Brown "yeeaaaoooohhhh!" It was just a yell. He was excited. He believed in his cause.

He was passionate about it. (In a strange turn of fate, I actually felt sorry for this guy.)

But the next day on the radio, Letterman and Leno, CNN and MTV, he was viciously lampooned for being out of control and as someone who had a problem with anger management. He was even interviewed by a member of the TV media establishment who repeatedly questioned him and his wife about his anger issues. The issue on trial *was not* that he let out a goofy yell. He can do *that*. Just look at the stands at any ball game. He could have yelled there and nobody would have blinked. What *was* on trial was Dean's ability to be passionate. Don't get me wrong. I thought it was a pretty funny yell myself but only because he looked goofy doing it.

Others laughed for the wrong reason. They hate passion. These are people who perceive passionate people as dangerous loose cannons. (And, by all means, we must make sure that our politicians never really stand for anything.) Passionate people are feared as being hair-triggered and unreliable. They are labeled angry, offensive, and bigoted because they take a stand.

Here's the problem. This fear has invaded many Christians and many of their churches. In an era where standing out is punished, many favor maintaining the status quo. *Christian people have become afraid of the world.* They are afraid to take a stand, and their souls are dying as a result. They have chosen the safety, ease, and services that meet their own needs and have forsaken the rough and rugged passion of the Cross. They have substituted comfort for adventure. They have traded the exciting, passion-filled life that is walked by faith for a stroll through a well-manicured, prepackaged garden of no surprises. To take a stand may cause pain. To bring passion may rock the boat.

Now, I'm not advocating a mindless passion just to get excited. People with passion not only scare people in the wrong direction but also motivate people down the wrong path. Misguided passion can give others the idea that you know something they don't know, and since you are passionate, you must be right. Mindless passion is misguided and leads to pain. I'm not trying to get everybody to simply "get excited."

Passion on the Rebound

But I do see glimmers of hope in the eyes of many Christians today. Passion may be on the rebound in some corners of our churches. This hope is driven by the fact that "Jesus Christ is the same yesterday and today and forever" (Heb. 13:8). The passionate and courageous still take Jesus at His word. What He has done in the past, He can do again. Their courage comes from being filled with the unquenchable holy fire of God's personal presence. And when the Spirit of God lights a person on fire from the inside out, he or she begins to see the world not as it is but as it could be. He or she begins to see new visions and dream new dreams. And the Christian life always must be lived with an eye toward God's dream, not our ideas for success and comfort. And really, deep down, pursuing this dream is the life you've always wanted.

In his book *Seizing Your Divine Moment,* Erwin McManus writes:

> We are all haunted with the fear of living lives of insignificance, and we all hear the voice that tells us we can live the dream. Somehow we all know that to play it safe is to lose the game. By definition an *adventure* is "an undertaking or enterprise of a hazardous nature." And life as God intended us to live it is nothing less than an adventure. It comes at great risk and at significant cost.[1]

Passionate dreaming will cost you something. You may lose friends and you may even change vocations. When you align yourself with Christ's dream for this world, you automatically begin to look at things differently from those around you. To be great will now require you to become small. To be invisible in the eyes of people must be preferred to being well known. To receive, you must first be willing to give. To be exalted you must become humble.

And, really, isn't this what you're hungering for? Don't you hunger for a world where godly people really act godly? Where spiritual leaders don't try to hog the spotlight and grind people into the ground as they try to help Christ build His Church? Where churches are a safe place for lost sheep and wounded people instead of museums and mausoleums for the already convinced?

Passion Is *Fire*

To be sure, I am convinced that our lives need a major infusion of passion. And passion is also known by another name. I like to call it fire. And in this context, let me show you what I mean by fire—as in getting "fired up"—or as they say in west Texas, "farred up."

I remember in ninth grade in Odessa, Texas, when our football team took the field before the kickoff, we would usually have this big pileup around the coach as he gave us his final instructions. We would jump around and scream and pat each other on the *backs*. (No fanny-patting was allowed in Odessa.) Now since I was never that great at football, I was usually on the outside part of the pack away from those who may actually need to hear those final instructions. But I still jumped around.

The point of this pileup was twofold. First, it was aimed at getting all of us fired up—the thought being the higher the emotional pitch, the better the hitting on the football field. (This is usually true.) The second point of the pack in my mind was to strike fear in the heart of the enemy. See—fired-up people may just do something crazy. And on the football field, there's nothing scarier than a crazy man with pads and helmet on. For a football player, the fire is empowering and frightening at the same time.

The same is true for us as Christ followers. When we have a godly fire in our souls and a godly passion for God's Word, His dream will empower us to live holy lives that are redemptive to a hurting world. Along with this, a godly fire puts our enemy on the run. He knows there is nothing scarier than a sold-out Christian, armed with the full armor of God. That's why the devil's play all along is to try to put that fire out before it gets started.

The Light of the World Is Not Fluorescent

In the Sermon on the Mount, Jesus made this simple statement, "You are the light of the world" (Matt. 5:14). Now, when He made that statement, He was talking to people, not lightning bugs. So what did He mean by *light*?

Well, think about it. They were still hundreds of years away from electric light. Jesus wasn't saying, "Go be light bulbs. Go make this pretty little even light. Go out and spread your little electric charges." He was saying, "You are the fire of the world." Everybody He spoke to that day would have understood what He meant, but that meaning gets lost on us because of the fluorescent world we live in.

Fire in that context gave light but also brought problems. Lay the torch next to the thatch roof, and you would have a problem. Put it in a bucket of water, and it would go out. If you forgot to keep it going, you would hope your friend still had some fire to share. Matches weren't around just yet. And if you have seen the movie *Castaway* or watched an episode of *Survivor*, you know just how hard it is to start a fire from scratch.

Jesus was telling the people, "Look—you are it. You are both fire *and* light. You illuminate the world so that people know the right way to live. You eliminate the power of darkness just by being you. But you also provide the fuel to begin a revolution of the soul. You are both fire *and* fire-starter."

Now this may sound a little strange to you. Maybe you liked it better when you thought Jesus was comparing us to a 60-watt bulb. Why would God liken us to fire in the first place?

Well, in the opening chapter of the Bible, God said, "Let us make man in our image, in our likeness" (Gen. 1:26).

This means that somehow we are made in the image of God. And all throughout the Bible God tells us various aspects of His character, the same character that we share as His image bearers. One specific reference in Heb. 12:29 says, "Our 'God is a consuming fire.'" So we are made in the image of God, and if we are Christians, we have His Holy Spirit within us. We are like fire, in God's image, and filled with fire. So we are both fire and fire-starter. We have the light within and without.

Since that is true, then the Christian life should be marked by this fire. It should be driven by a relentless pursuit, a passion, to re-create God's original dream for His creation. Our lives should echo the Lord's Prayer to do our part when Jesus said, "May your will be done here on earth, just as it is in heaven" (Matt. 6:10, NLT). Christian people should both illuminate and motivate. Your fire should spread just by the way you speak and by who you speak about.

So let me get back to my story. After my holy encounter with God that October day, I still waffled. I tried to talk Him out of it. I saw all the obstacles and forgot about His power. I understood how Gideon felt when the first fleece came back with the answer he didn't like. I was thinking, *God, are You sure? I have a lot to lose if I quit my job.* Finally, in a moment of total surrender, I accepted God's invitation to spread the fire to all who would listen as a lifetime vocational calling.

Oddly, my wife, Mindy, wasn't shocked when I brought her the news. She had also been dealing with God on the idea of surrendering to His fire. God was letting her know that if she would be obedient and pursue this new course, all her dreams for a bigger family would be fulfilled. God gave her Scripture promises that showed her that this was the right thing to do—and she believed.

So in a big step of faith, which turned out better than we could have imagined, I quit my relatively successful business career, and Mindy went back to work. I went back to seminary while she paid all the bills. This was a total team effort from the start, and I thank God for sending me such a great wife. She is still my biggest supporter and torch carrier.

After that, God led us to begin a new church in Tulsa, Oklahoma, through the support and prodding of my mentor and friend, Dave McKellips. We launched this church in September 2000 and have loved every minute of it since. We have seen firsthand the passion it takes to ignite previously passionless people. We have had the great opportunity to help start fires inside of people who have been burned out and broken.

I am convinced more than ever that once people feel the heat and burn within, they'll never be the same. I remember the old story about young John Wesley, who would eventually become the founder of the Methodist movement and a mighty hero of the faith. He had returned to England from a missionary trip to the Native American population on the eastern seaboard of what is now the United States. It didn't go very well, and he felt like a failure. He was doing all the right things for God, but he lacked something. As the story goes, one night he heard a preacher reading aloud from Luther's preface to the Book of Romans. During this reading Wesley stated, "I felt my heart strangely warmed. I felt I did trust in Christ, Christ alone for salvation; and an assurance was given me that He had taken away my sins, even mine, and saved me from the law of sin and death."[2]

After that night, everything changed for Wesley. To me, it sounds a lot like the arrows that hit me in the chest on the Mall in Washington, D.C. The warmth was the fire; the arrows were the fire.

God's fire is like that. It's unmistakable and unforgettable. It makes a lifelong impression on the recipient, but it never stops there. God's fire bearers know how to start a fire and keep it stoked in themselves and in others. They are the light of the world, the city on the hill that can't be hidden.

You know the people with the fire by the way things change after they leave the scene. You still smell their smoke on the ones they have touched. You still see their godly influence long after they are gone.

Our culture needs some godly people to pick up the torch. Our churches need a fresh vision to overcome the apathy and complacency we live with. We need some people to begin to bear the image of their Father God, the Consuming Fire.

But fire alone is not as good as fire together. Fire together conserves warmth, but fire separated can quickly lose its heat. Anyone who has had hot chocolate in a Styrofoam cup on a cold Friday night at a football game knows that the heat quickly leaves the cup if you don't drink it fast enough (which is impossible without scalding the back of your throat). And anyone who wants to put out a campfire slowly knows to spread out the coals so that they no longer touch and share their warmth. Hot coals on their own will quickly succumb to burnout and lose their heat.

Conserving temperature is what we call insulation. For instance, a Thermos is built to conserve what a paper cup will quickly lose. The Thermos has a conservation mind-set. I heard an unknown voice on the radio once say, "Thermos keeps the hot stuff hot and the cold stuff cold. *How does it know?*" A home has foam in its walls to keep warmth where it belongs. Insulation creates a needed temperature barrier between hot things and cold things so that they stay at the desired temperature longer.

Here's what I've found to be true. Chasing cool *isolates,* but chasing Christ *insulates.* Chasing cool will force you to try to stand out from the pack at all costs and do your own thing, while chasing Christ will automatically include a love for His Body.

It's interesting to note the rapid move I have seen in our Church culture away from having ties to a local church body. Even Christians who attended regular worship meetings in the past and were actively involved in some way are giving it all up for a church on the Web or some preacher on TV. They're separating themselves and making themselves more vulnerable than they know. Their heat is leaving, and they don't even feel it. This isolation is showing itself in real-life symptoms. One of the frequent complaints I hear most often is that people don't have any Christian friends. And consequently one of the biggest problems facing churches today is the malady known as clinical depression.

As you may know, clinical depression is usually

treated in two ways: first, through continuing talks with a therapist and, second, with medication. The first is insulation. It's good to have people to talk to. We need to talk and be heard. This keeps our soul warm. But I'm afraid of the negative effects of the second form of treatment. I know sometimes only chemicals can help people through depression. I am not against the use of drugs to accomplish a godly purpose and believe these drugs are a gift from God for those who have no other way to healing. But I feel that one of the reasons our churches lack the fire and passion of days gone by is that we're medicating ourselves away from our passion and fire.

Many prescription antidepressants are handed out for everything nowadays. Have a bad day? Get on drugs. Dad was mean to you? Better medicate that. Got spankings instead of time-outs as a child? Sounds like a good day for Prozac. And what these particular kinds of drugs do is the same thing a pail of water does to a campfire. They keep emotions, both good and bad, from burning out of control; they take away the peaks and valleys. In the end these drugs produce just what our world needs—more people who don't care about anything very much. Take a look inside churches in the United States, and you'll see pews full of people who just don't care. They're physically and chemically unable to care.

Now for some cases of depression, the only answer is to regulate the chemical known as serotonin. As I mentioned earlier, I am all for using medication in the proper place. But in many other cases, all that needs to be done is for a person to become more a part of the Body of Christ. Jesus always said it was better to give than to receive, that somehow we get a better life by sharing our lives with others.

So how about sharing your heat? People need *your* fire. They need *your* heat. And you need theirs. Don't let the bad fires in life deter you from continuing to make the effort. All of us have been burned while trying to warm others. But those scars are no deeper than those our Savior bore for us. He cared enough to share His fire with those who would ultimately betray and burn Him. He shared His life with men who would deny Him. He ate meals with the worst sort of people and hung out with those society had left to cool on the shelf. He modeled a life of fire and passion for others, and He invites us to care about Him enough to do the same.

And Jesus would have worn a park ranger's hat.

6

HUMAN CHAIN

Choosing Connection over Competition

Greater love has no one than this, that he lay down his life for his friends (John 15:13).

OK, I have an honest confession. This may sound odd, and I can't believe I'm telling this to many of you who are total strangers. I mean, we don't know each other that well, and your opinion of me does matter. But I have to speak from my heart and bare my true soul since I'm on this road to recovery, no matter how disturbing it may sound.

So here it is in recovery format: "My name is Brett Rickey, a grateful believer in Jesus Christ, and I really *like* watching the Weather Channel." Mmm—hmm. Sorry. It's not an addiction, just kind of an obsession. I really mean it. I dig Doppler radar and satellite imagery from space and the in-depth personal analysis and sheer human life-and-death drama that you see on the Weather Channel, every hour, with your local forecast on the "eights." I'm breathless at the mention of the Fujita scale. (That's the F-1 through F-5 power ratings given to tornadoes.) I'm awestruck by the men and women who risk their lives chasing these killer storms. They are the kind of crazy that you just have to love out loud! I truly find it fascinating, and I know I may have a problem. But there you go. I've finally admitted it. (Why is step one so hard?)

I know such an admission may keep me from speaking in certain places, because most would agree that the Weather Channel is not cool. It's a place frequented by storm chasers and hurricane hunters, but not those looking for anything remotely cool. I mean, hey, they do try, but most meteorologists are just too smart to be cool—which, when you think about it, is the way you want your weather. You don't need *attitude* when getting the forecast, just the facts. And the Weather Channel is dominated by one topic: the weather.

Now my friend Brad used to be a radio DJ, and he doesn't care about the weather because he had to give the temperature and forecast six times per hour for three hours a day for 18 years. Brad is definitely cooler than me. Cool people usually look as though they don't care about stuff, even if they do. Brad looks like that—as though he could be from a smart place like Philadelphia but isn't.

So I like to know the weather. I'm captivated by cold fronts and their effect on warm moist air and why lightning happens and where tornadoes are going to form. Did you know that scientists still aren't really sure why lightning happens at all? It's true. They have theories, but they aren't proven. I heard it on the Discovery Channel, TWC's more scientific cousin. I'm bordering on an addiction but have yet to face any kind of intervention from friends.

On the Weather Channel they always show where the flooding rain is happening. And they always have these videos showing this bewildered person standing on the roof of a car with his or her dog, waiting to be rescued after driving a Volkswagen into five feet of moving water. I want to yell at those people and say, "Don't you watch the Weather Channel? You never drive your car into moving water! If you do, you end up looking stupid on TV." But of course, they don't think the Weather Channel is cool, so they end up on TV.

Sometimes there isn't a helicopter to rescue the victims in a flood. They may be hanging from a limb or in a tree and people will throw something at them to pull them to shore. But the coolest thing I have seen is when all these people who don't appear to know each other lock their arms, wade into dangerous water, and form a human chain to get these non-Weather Channel watchers out of harm's way. That is weather excitement at its best. Real reality TV before the genre was invented.

But this kind of weather drama also shows humanity at their best, and that's what I would like to explore. See, I believe that inside each person there is a God-given, noble strain that wants to step up and help those in danger, no matter the personal cost. All of this is just a click away on the Weather Channel!

I saw it personally in the aftermath of the Oklahoma City bombing in April 1995. I lived there at the time and was working five miles away. I saw the plume of heavy black smoke and heard the stories of damage and headed downtown. I don't know why, but I just felt that I might be able to help. I wanted to help. I needed to help.

After making my way toward the Murrah Building,

going against the flow of stunned faces and weeping mothers and broken glass and concrete, I saw the bloody, dust-covered victims being led away to places of healing. I saw the ATF and FBI agents just standing there, uncertain of how to proceed. I heard the rumor that flowed through the crowd that another bomb was found and saw everyone run in terror. That included me. I wasn't much help that day. There was really nothing I could have done. When I got home and watched the news, I wondered why somebody would be so cruel.

But another thing I saw impressed me. All of Oklahoma City rallied, as did other parts of the United States. There were miles of cars of people who wanted to give blood. Everybody wanted to be a part of the human chain to rescue their fellow human beings. Firemen came from all over the country to help them dig out. Ambulances came from all over Oklahoma and lined up waiting for the survivors to be pulled from the rubble. Sadly, the ambulances sat empty as there weren't any survivors found after the initial wave. The tragedy was staggering, and the sadness touched everyone. As I watched a 10th anniversary show in 2005, I wept again as I remembered the images of rising smoke and the smell of burning cars. I remembered watching the great people giving of themselves to try to save their friends. Even fallen humanity, Christian and non-Christian, full of a sin nature that they were born with, can somehow rise above it all when the cause is saving another human life. People are at their best when they are in rescue mode. When people are under the rubble or in dangerous water, nothing else matters except getting them out. All other appointments are secondary when life-and-death matters are in your face. This is the greater love that Jesus spoke of. And we were born to let that love flow to others.

I think that's why Jesus ended His ministry on earth by challenging His disciples with something that would give them a life vision. He had shown them that the best use of a life is to give it away. Then He said this to them: "Go and make disciples of all nations, baptizing them in the name of the Father and of the Son and of the Holy Spirit, and teaching them to obey everything I have commanded you. And surely I am with you always, to the very end of the age" (Matt. 28:19-20).

Now I am not going to give a full commentary on these verses. Others have spent their lives writing books about the beauty and meaning of this scripture. But look at it in the context of being part of a human chain and the excitement people feel and the reckless abandon necessary to pull people from the rubble in life. Jesus was issuing them a reason to live, or as Rick Warren might say, he was giving them their life mission. Here's my question. Why do so many people in churches today, who own this mission, look bored? (That would include pastors.) Why does it seem that the church in the United States seems to be off-message? Those people who were working in the rubble in Oklahoma City weren't bored. They were intense. Their movements had purpose. But I don't see that a lot in church.

Now I like church people. I have gone to church my whole life, becoming a Christian at age 5. My father, Norman, has been preaching since his early 20s. He's now 83 and still going strong. Without the church, I don't know where I would be. Here's the truth I have found. The churches that understand these verses and live by them are usually fun places to attend. There is life and purpose in corporate worship times and small groups. Everybody is forming a human chain for the purpose of making disciples.

But I have also been in churches where the people know this verse in their heads but somehow are able to look at the rubble and not make a move. They all agree that people in the rubble need a hand up, not a hand out, and that somebody *should* do something. But they never do anything. Oh, they sing songs praising God, maybe even raising their holy hands, but they never do any digging, and the people continue to stay trapped. They never form a human chain, so the people around them continue to stay buried or drown in the flood of materialism and selfishness that characterizes our world.

To me, this is where the church is missing it so badly and why we remain irrelevant to the culture. We are on-message in many ways, but we are not doing much to be the visible Body of Christ. Peter encouraged those first believers by saying, "Be careful how you live among your unbelieving neighbors. Even if they accuse you of doing wrong, they will see your honorable behavior, and they will believe and give honor to God when he comes to judge the world" (1 Pet. 2:12, NLT).

When unbelievers see real love in action, they take notice. And this verse says that they will believe. It's really fun when people begin to connect with each other, and through that connection, they make a visible statement to the world that says, "If you need help, we will be there." That's how passion spreads. That's how the fire really gets going. But most people don't see light shining from Christians—they see anger.

So many Christian leaders on TV are always mad at things. They want to picket everything and tell you how bad the world is and how mean the world is being to the Christian community. They make Jesus look bad by being mad all the time. I never remember Jesus and His disciples picketing or boycotting, and their world was full of social injustice. Jesus actually reserved His harsh words for those who were supposed to be God's people. He expected people living in the dark to act like it. Why do all these Christian leaders get mad at the darkness for acting like darkness? I guess it's just easier to throw stones at the problem than it is to get busy and solve it by being the light that the world really needs.

Now I'm not implying that we should stay out of social or governmental affairs, just that we don't need to yell at those far from God *for* being far from God. We need to be introspective with our criticism and love those outside of the faith. I mean, really, if you were not a follower of Christ, and all you saw of Christians were the angry people on TV, would you want to join up and follow that? Godly passion lets others see love in action, not just talking heads that tell you how righteous their cause is.

Now, godly passion is something that shouldn't exist in isolation. As I said earlier, the pursuit of cool over Christ will cost you money, health, family, friends, and ultimately your soul.

The pursuit of cool is a self-dominated lifestyle that isolates. The cool lifestyle is the chase of something that can't be defined; therefore it can never be attained. And as soon as something *is* cool, it lasts for about an hour and then vanishes. But another thing that hurts when you chase cool is that the pursuit of cool is really hard on other people. Here's what I mean.

When we chase cool, other people are *the competition.* Think about it a minute. We have to dress better, smell better, look better, and act snobbier than our fellow cool chasers. Because not just anybody can be cool, you see, only the special. The pursuit of cool is driven by the need to be noticed and to stand out, no matter what it costs. It's totally self-centered.

But the Christian life is supposed to be the opposite. I say *supposed to be* because many times it isn't. So why is it that chasing cool still happens in the church? I believe if we are going to keep from chasing cool and then continue to pursue Christ, we are going to need help from other people we trust to evaluate what we are really chasing and be open enough to invite their feedback when they see something out of line. We will need a human chain when we fall back into the river of self-deception. We will need somebody to get the rocks off of our head when our self-centered world implodes. We will need to learn to choose connection over competition.

That sounds noble, doesn't it? But it's not easy. Because other people still bug us. In a poem attributed to Mother Teresa titled "Anyway," there's a line telling us to love people even though they are selfish and difficult. How do we do that when people can really rub us the wrong way?

The apostle Paul addresses how we should live together as a human chain in his letter to the Galatians. It gives us some really practical advice about living in a connected community, and I want to look at four of his ideas that may help.

1. First, to live in this connected community, I must learn to treat fellow Christians as teammates. True teammates know that they have to do their part or the whole team loses. Cool chasers don't have a team mentality. It's not that they are bad people. Many of them come to church. But they don't have a good concept of why God left them here, so they compete. Paul begins chapter 6 by saying, "Dear friends, if another Christian is overcome by some sin, you who are godly should gently and humbly help that person back onto the right path. And be careful not to fall into the same temptation yourself" (Gal. 6:1, NLT).

In Paul's world, Christians were still susceptible to sin. In other words, even though they saw the high water in life—God's directive against certain practices—they drove their VW in the middle anyway and were crying for help. He says that when people sin, a human chain must be formed.

Look at those words *gently* and *humbly*. What's the

first thing you need to hear when you have messed up? Gentle words or harsh ones? Do you really need somebody to tell you how not to do it again? When we fall, it's much nicer to hear a kind word than a rebuke. The rebuke can come later, but when it is rescue time, all you want is out of the mess.

The Greek word that was translated as *overcome* comes from a word that means "slip up," as on ice. You thought you could walk on it, but you couldn't. It was sin, but it was an accidental-type sin.

Growing up, I played sports all my life. And sometimes somebody would let the team down, like striking out with the bases loaded or missing an easy lay-up. In sports, you learn to go to that person and say, "Hey—keep your head up. It's going to be OK."

Football players pat each other on the back (or other places). Gymnasts hug each other a lot. Good teammates are there to help the others up when they are down—not kick them. In 2006 the Dallas Cowboys learned this the hard way. They hired a talented but troubled wide receiver named Terrell Owens. Terrell had a history of being a bad teammate—always blaming others and not being an encourager—but the Cowboys took the chance that he could be changed because he was such a good player. It turns out that he hasn't changed and his attitude has affected the entire team negatively.

In the Church, sometimes we are good at criticizing and blaming but not at helping each other up when we fall. I've heard people say things like, "Well, I saw that coming." "He's getting what he deserves." "Next time you need to ask me before you do something so stupid." And these are the same people who do nothing to alleviate the problem. They don't see their fellow Christian as a teammate; they see him or her as a competitor in some kind of spiritual derby. Verse 2 shows a team mentality, "Share each other's troubles and problems, and in this way obey the law of Christ" (NLT).

Unfortunately, here in the United States our spirituality is all about me and my intimacy with God. As long as I'm doing OK, then everything else is secondary. But what if we really saw all Christians belonging to a team? Not our team, but Jesus' team? See, in sports if one member of a team doesn't perform, everyone suffers. If the catcher can't catch, the pitcher is wasting his or her time. If the quarterback can't throw, the receivers are not going to catch a ball. In sports, you are only as good as your weakest link. And if one member of the team isn't doing well, the whole team rallies to make sure that one person picks up the slack. That's the way the Church should be. My local church is just a small part of Jesus' team, but all believers are on it.

So let me ask you this hard question: what if you

began to view your relationship with Christ as dependent on how well others related to Him? For example, if you're doing well but your buddies are stinking it up, then you aren't doing so well after all. Hmm—that's not a very American way to look at things, is it? In the United States we believe in accepting Christ as our "personal Savior." (Although the Bible never really uses that term.) Now hear me right. I do believe that you and I are ultimately responsible to God for our own lives. But I also believe that you can't live the Christian life without accepting responsibility for doing your part on the team you're elected to play on.

In the Old Testament the Israelites understood the team concept. Smart people tell me it's a very Eastern mind kind of thing. Whereas we in the United States (or *the West*) see things as all about me, Eastern-minded folk like the Jewish people see things as all about *we*.

To highlight this *we* kind of thinking, God gave us this story about a guy named Achan who sinned. And because of his sin, God was angry, and his whole nation was punished. "But the Israelites acted unfaithfully in regard to the devoted things; Achan son of Carmi, the son of Zimri, the son of Zerah, of the tribe of Judah, took some of them. So the LORD's anger burned against Israel" (Josh. 7:1).

Do you see what happened in this paragraph? God

sees sin in His people as a group thing, a team thing. And God understands that if one person on the team takes a break, everybody gets hurt. Achan was only one man, but God dealt with the whole. This is a really chilling story to me. But it gets to the heart of how important our connection is, no matter how much we choose to be individualists.

If you really start to see the Christian life as a team sport, you'll pick up the team member who has fallen and try to help him or her get better. Because if he or she gets better, then so does your team, and your team wins. If a teammate falls into sin, help him or her up; don't berate the teammate. If a teammate is sick, visit him or her until health returns. If a teammate is in financial trouble, help him or her out. When a teammate needs help, lend a hand, and you drive your team to victory. And when you do this, guess what happens. Peter says, "They will believe and give honor to God when he comes to judge the world" (1 Pet. 2:12, NLT). And that's the point of the mission Jesus gave us. To make more disciples: as a team.

Paul gets a little testy with individualized faith. "If you think you are too important to help someone in need, you are only fooling yourself. You are really a nobody" (Gal. 6:3, NLT). Now, I know many people who read their Bibles a lot and never help anyone in need. This shouldn't be.

I guess I like the word *tribe* rather than *team* when describing spiritual stuff. Maybe it's because the reality TV show *Survivor* uses that word. Anyway, a tribe is a group of families with a common ancestry or heritage. When a member of the tribe fights, it's everybody's fight. God didn't create us to be spiritual islands where we sit around basking in His presence getting spiritual sunburn so the world could look at us and see how holy we are. God created us to reflect His glory so that they could see *us* and thereby see *Him.* Here's a saying God gave me, *Competition isolates, but connection insulates.* To live in this connected community, I must learn to treat fellow Christians as teammates.

2. Second, if you see your life as part of a team, you have to learn to play your position. "Be sure to do what you should, for then you will enjoy the personal satisfaction of having done your work well, and you won't need to compare yourself to anyone else. For we are each responsible for our own conduct" (vv. 4-5, NLT). Highlight the words "what you should." In other words, there are some things you should and should not do.

As Rick Warren states in *The Purpose-Driven Life,* one of your five purposes in life is to have a ministry to other believers. Every one of us is a minister.[1] We can minister God's love anytime we want. Paul says that if you do this, you won't need to compare yourself to other people. You can quit competing. Look at verse 5. "For we are each responsible for our own conduct" (NLT).

One day God will look all of us in the eye and ask, "What did you do with your life?" Unfortunately, our responses may look like, "Well, see, I was really busy making money for my family. Well, see, I was so stressed just trying to make ends meet. Well, see, I really didn't have any worthwhile talent that You needed, God." And He will say, "Really, now. That's not how I see it."

But sometimes, you get it right and help people out. Then here's another big trick of the devil that happens once you start to do ministry. You start noticing all the other people who do what you do. And instead of rejoicing for what God has given them to do, you get jealous if they do it better or, more important, if they get more credit for doing their part.

Doesn't it seem unjust when people get credit and you don't for doing the same thing? Don't you hate that? Recognition is dangerous because it can lead to pride, but a lack of recognition is even more painful because it can lead to jealousy and eventually bitterness. And jealousy is always driven by competition, not connection.

Before I became a pastor, I had spent 11 years in a competitive business environment where people tried to get other people's customers to choose their product instead. I was so glad to get out of that environment. I looked forward to hanging out with other pastors, talking strategy, and finding better ways for our team to help dig people out of the rubble. I honestly thought of my fellow pastors as teammates. But they don't all agree on that point with me. In fact, one of the saddest things I have had to learn is that pastors are really competitive for each other's sheep. They like to be number 1 and the "it" guy or gal. And they see other churches as the competition instead of part of their own team.

I hate this about the formal ministry. It turns people into salesmen for their way instead of God's way. It makes pastors jealous when a big giver leaves their congregation. Not because of the love for the person but because of the lost money they drop into the plate on Sundays at the other church. This is competition at its worst.

The competition is also driven in the pews. Attendees hear of the great things going on at the other churches and want to bring that to their own place, regardless of whether or not God thinks it's a good idea. They press their pastor to bring changes to the music, the youth group, the facility, or the color of the carpet, all in an attempt to bring the cool way to their church. God rarely gets a consult on such ideas.

If you truly value connection over competition, you

will be the first to honor the teammate who gets the accolades. If you understand that you're a winner too, all the better. And if God's team wins, we all win. Many good people struggle here. It always alarms me at how easily jealousy comes into the church. Paul wrote, "Let us not become conceited, or irritate one another, or be jealous of one another" (Gal. 5:26, NLT).

François de La Rochefoucauld wrote, "In jealousy there is more self-love than love." Boy, isn't *that* true? Jealousy shows others who we really are. And if you feel it, others will see it.

3. Third, if you want to choose connection, then stay true to your team. *If you choose cool over connection, there is a high cost.* "Don't be misled. Remember that you can't ignore God and get away with it. You will always reap what you sow! Those who live only to satisfy their own sinful desires will harvest the consequences of decay and death. But those who live to please the Spirit will harvest everlasting life from the Spirit" (6:7-8, NLT).

A lot of good spiritual people think this sowing and reaping thing applies to money—at least if you watch TV preachers, that is. Sowing in this context is more than giving—it's a lifestyle. And whatever you plant in life will sprout somewhere—sometimes in places you don't expect.

When you choose to stay true to the team and sow good seeds, it comes down to two things: words and deeds. Let me focus a minute on words on the team. The sin of gossip is almost like one of those things we wink at. It's like something we do, but we just can't help ourselves, so we justify it and call it something new. For instance, instead of saying we're gossiping, we're really giving prayer requests or showing concern. It's always good to gossip with a little frown on your face. You know, be sincere-looking.

But gossip is really deadly because it works by putting others down in an attempt to elevate you. Author Donald Miller talks about the reason we do this in his book *Searching for God Knows What*. He likens our existence to being in a lifeboat full of one too many people, and in order for the whole group to survive, somebody must be tossed out of the boat. He believes we live our lives so that we get to maintain our position in the lifeboat and don't get tossed out. And when we gossip, we try to elevate ourselves so that we are not in last place in the boat. Gossip is the natural outgrowth of a world living in the lifeboat.[2] We will always try to separate ourselves from others when we see others as the competition instead of partners in the human chain.

Anger is another danger to the team spirit. Nobody likes to play with a hothead. Have you seen those commercials that advertise the miracle memory-foam mattresses? On one end of the mattress they set a glass full of juice. On the other end is a lady jumping up and down on the mattress. The miracle is that while she's hopping up and down, the juice never spills. I think I would like that kind of mattress. But then I thought of this word picture from Proverbs, "A gentle answer turns away wrath, but harsh words stir up anger" (15:1, NLT).

Now this is one of those no-brainer Proverbs. We know it's true every time, but we have a hard time putting it into action, because when people talk in a certain tone, we tend to mirror it. If they're mad, we get mad. If they talk loudly, we tend to want to talk louder. But what if we became memory-foam kind of people? It is possible, you know. When people are hopping mad, you don't have to spill over and react in anger. Even good teammates can make you mad, but you still have a choice. So remain calm, and learn to choose your words carefully. If you do, everybody will sleep better in the process.

See—we are not an exclusive club; we are an inclusive team. Anybody can play on God's team. And if you'll play and stay true to your team, you are guaranteed to win. The end of the Bible describes how our team wins! Even with me and you playing on it. And some of us aren't that bright—even on our good days.

Did you hear the story about the guy who sees a frog on the road that says, "Kiss me, and I'll be a princess"? He puts the frog in his pocket and keeps walking. Frustrated, she asks, "Why won't you kiss me? If you will, I'll be your princess." He takes the frog out of his pocket and replies, "Listen—I'm a computer geek, and I don't have time for a girlfriend. But a talking frog is cool."

Even though you and I are not that smart, God still wants us on His team anyway. That encourages a guy like me. Stay true to God's team, walk with His Spirit, and—

4. Finish the game! "So don't get tired of doing what is good. Don't get discouraged and give up, for we will reap a harvest of blessing at the appropriate time. Whenever we have the opportunity, we should do good to everyone, especially to our Christian brothers and sisters" (Gal. 6:9-10, NLT).

Many of you have been Christians for years, but you're coasting. What once burned isn't burning. You used to be in the game, giving it everything, but for some reason, you bailed. Paul says we can't quit. *We have to play as if it's literally the fourth quarter.* The game is not over—we can't get tired. We have wounded players out on the battlefield. We have stranded motorists stuck on their way in life. We have people under the rubble who need a human chain to pull them out.

It's still a war, and our enemy wants to destroy the Church. We don't have the choice of playing it safe if we really want to win—our families are at stake. We can't keep chasing cool. It's an idol. We can't keep competing with other Christians. We're on the same team! We must embrace the message of Jesus when He prayed, "My prayer for all of them is that they will be one, just as you and I are one, Father" (John 17:21, NLT).

It's fun to compete in games that don't mean much. But life is too important to compete with the team you should be playing on. Take this chapter as your challenge to begin to look for other Christians to share your life and your life's work with. Don't be satisfied until you find a church home where people really view their lives as rescuers, not spectators. Our team wins! And you won't want to miss the party after the game.

7

JESUS IS BETTER THAN SUPERMAN

The Answer to Soul Kryptonite

God is love. Whoever lives in love lives in God, and God in him (1 John 4:16).

Every little boy grows up wanting to be bigger and tougher and faster than everybody else in the neighborhood. Boys like to win and for people to know they are good at stuff. Picking a young boy last in a sandlot football game, even though we didn't understand it at the time, was like handing him a guaranteed ticket to therapy as an adult. We want to be the hero, not the afterthought or the infamous "player to be named later" in a sports trade. We want to make our mark and make sure nobody forgets about us. I think this is the way God wired us.

So boys grow up looking for heroes to pattern their lives after. And comic book people know this stuff inside and out. One of the greatest characters ever written for comic books is the guy from the planet Krypton called Superman, also known as Clark Kent. I grew up as a fan of the 1950s black-and-white TV version of Superman. I didn't have time for comic books.

George Reeves played the lead as the strong man in dark gray tights. Physically, George was not at all buff by our standards today and looked nothing like the comic book drawings. But he was probably a formidable figure compared to the smallish heroes of his day on television. Today one of the supermen of my generation is the governor of California. He's known by a variation of his first name, simply "Ahh-nuldd!"

The creators of Superman did us a great service by making Clark Kent a little more like the rest of us when they allowed him to be allergic to this green rock they called kryptonite. Whenever kryptonite got on or near Superman, he would go weak in the knees faster than a group of 16-year-old boys ogling Jessica Simpson in her "Daisy Dukes." Kryptonite was the only thing that could stop Superman. Kryptonite made him normal and very nonheroic. It kept him earthbound and in a great deal of personal agony. And once the evil villain Lex Luthor found out his weakness, the balance of power shifted and the game was on. Lex now knew that Superman was vulnerable and that his glory could be destroyed by something that Superman couldn't control. Superman had an inner weakness to this mysterious green rock that his enemy now would exploit.

Sound familiar? Let me give you a short doctrinal talk, and then I'll get to the point. This is a very superficial treatment of issues that take volumes to adequately explain, but here is the CliffsNotes version as I understand it. (I have never met Cliff, but I think I would like him.)

Since the fall of humanity, our enemy has done a great job of identifying and then preying on our own inward bent toward self-idolization and corresponding self-destruction. Theologians call this inherent tendency to sin, or inner weakness, our sinful nature. All of us since Adam have been born with a sinful nature, and this in turn makes us vulnerable to any sin. It is our native language from birth. Nobody has to teach anybody how to sin. My three-year-old daughter, Hope, has never been taught to disobey, but she does it well. It's instinctive. And it's not her fault. Just like she was born with curly blonde hair that makes her cuter than, well, your child—she knows how to sin well.

Not only are we sinners by nature, but we are also sinners by practice. The Bible says, "All have sinned and fall short of the glory of God" (Rom. 3:23). Every person has sinned—even Billy Graham. But the Bible affirms that if we become Christ followers and accept His love and forgiveness, we have a new motivation for life from now through eternity. We call this salvation. We are thoroughly transformed and are given a new desire to love God and please Him. We are free to bring the life and truth of God where we work and eat and live because it is fully alive in us. God begins to change our inner nature and redeems what our enemy has sought to destroy—namely, our heart. And in the Holiness tradition, we can see this work of inner cleansing as being completed by the Holy Spirit. He transforms our nature, and we accept it by faith. When we were saved, we got all of God; but now as our hearts are fully cleansed by the Holy Spirit, we offer Him all of ourselves without reservation.

History proves that even a believer with a heart fully devoted to God is capable of sin as grotesque as any unrepentant heart. No believer is immune to self-deception and willful sin. Self-deception will lead us to hold on to our sin. And if we hold on to sin, our spiritual strength will evaporate faster than a mud puddle in Phoenix.

So here's the super point of this super discussion. Sin in the life of a believer is like kryptonite to Superman. Sin is literally soul kryptonite. And religious people are just as susceptible to this as anyone else. As Jesus pointed out in the Sermon on the Mount in Matt. 5—7, sin is not just an external matter. The Pharisees in His day were professionals at acting right, getting their external life OK for public viewing. But their internal thinking was wrong. They had sin in their soul. Everybody looked at them as having the best relationship with God, because they seemed really righteous. But Jesus knew better. He knew that people have to deal with the sin within before they can deal with the sin outside.

So let's get back to Clark Kent (Superman). What does Clark do when presented with kryptonite? Most of the time, he weakly runs the other direction if possible. He suddenly begins to look very human; a lot like me after 30 minutes running on the treadmill. But at least Clark knows he needs to run. I'm afraid many times we humans aren't as bright. So what do many Christ followers do when their soul is infected with a pattern of willful sin? Hmm—I'm afraid many are not as smart as Clark. God wants us to be spiritual supermen—but we like to play with kryptonite.

Here are a few of the wrong ways we sometimes deal with soul kryptonite, or sin.

1. Call it something nice. When we do have those moments of introspection and are confronted by God's light in an area we don't want to change, sometimes we change its name to protect our innocence. To call something a sin is a little ugly and judgmental, don't you think? So we call sin by other names. Let's call it tolerance. Maybe call it a learning experience or just an experiment. Nothing that others don't do, and they do it way more often. When we call our sin by another name, we can feel justified, because there's always somebody out there doing things worse than we are and therefore we don't have to do anything about it.

2. Avoid God's attention. It only took the first humans three chapters to get to this one. Look at what happened after Adam and Eve sinned the first sin, "Then the man and his wife heard the sound of the LORD God as he was walking in the garden in the cool of the day, and they hid from the LORD God among the trees of the garden. But the LORD God called to the man, 'Where are you?' He answered, 'I heard you in the garden, and I was afraid because I was naked; so I hid'" (Gen. 3:8-10).

OK, this picture brings to mind playing hide-and-seek with my girls. The younger ones think when they cover their face behind the couch that I can't see their backside sticking out into plain view. We do this same thing with God. We try to hide out until the coast is clear—only the coast doesn't clear the way we think it should. Maybe if God doesn't see us for a while, He'll forget, or better yet, maybe *we'll* forget. Come to think of it, maybe that's why we avoid God's attention so much. It's not that He can't forgive us, because we know that He can. I think most Christians have an idea that God's grace is inexhaustible because we know our own capacity to sin is too. But I think it's the power that shame holds on us for breaking our Father's heart and going back on our promises to Him.

I have the opportunity to talk with a lot of friends who are going through recovery for some of the addictions they are battling. And the biggest thing for any of them to get over is always the shame. They can accept forgiveness, they understand God's love, but they just have a hard time not feeling like losers, so they just hide out from God. When we run from God, we also tend to ignore what we did. I think Adam and Eve would have ignored that sin forever if God hadn't confronted them with the truth.

3. Redefine *sin*. Since we like to do it, and we are

good people, it can't be sin, so we change our definition of *sin* to fit our behavior. In the Old Testament, Saul was a character who chose to define *sin* in other ways, and it got him into big trouble and ultimately God's removal of blessing.

4. Get out the Novocain. We just get numb to the idea that what we are doing is wrong. We sin and keep sinning on purpose and our consciences get numb and we quit feeling the pain in our soul and quit seeing the pain we are causing others. In the apostle Paul's day, people began to speak for God, but they were not telling the truth. And after a while, they didn't even notice the lies they were telling. Paul called them "hypocritical liars, whose consciences have been seared as with a hot iron" (1 Tim. 4:2).

Boy, I never want a seared conscience, do you? It sounds painful. But it's unfortunately really common. In counseling with folks who are preparing to divorce, I see it all the time. They begin to numb themselves to the idea that their neglect in the marriage has been wrong and that divorce is really a sin. They have lied to themselves over and over, and now that still, small voice of God is drowned out by the screaming loud voice of "Me, me, me!"

See—all of us have areas of tenderness in our soul where we hear God's voice really clearly. But it's the areas where we're numb that really can do the most harm. Ever try to eat a cheeseburger after you get a tooth filled, before the numbness has worn off? You can eat a piece of your cheek if you aren't careful.

If we choose these wrong ways of dealing with sin, we become liars and hypocrites. Then, inevitably, we start to wear the religious mask that is so evident to everyone else but invisible to the wearer. It's the mask that drives unbelievers from considering the faith. It's the mask worn by the Pharisees in Jesus' day and in our day as well. I love the little proverb that says, "Blessed are those who have a tender conscience, but the stubborn are headed for serious trouble" (Prov. 28:14, NLT). *The* serious trouble is spiritual weakness and interpersonal conflicts.

Thankfully, David gives us a great breakdown of this whole confessional process. Here are a few things he suggests that we find in Ps. 32. He wants us to live like people who feel super, not like frightened children hiding behind the couch. But first, listen to his description of living with unconfessed sin: "When I refused to confess my sin, I was weak and miserable, and I groaned all day long. Day and night your hand of discipline was heavy on me. My strength evaporated like water in the summer heat" (vv. 3-4, NLT). *Sounds* like kryptonite, doesn't it?

So what's the best way to deal with sin?

1. First, we have to learn to call things what they really are. A sin is sin. You need to learn what it is and call it what it is. There are a couple kinds of sins, things we do and things we don't do that we should. The first is known as *sins of commission*—falling short of God's ideal by not obeying a known law of God. Two helpful passages of Scripture to help us identify these kinds of sin are found in God's top 10 lists in Exod. 20, and from the Sermon on the Mount in Matt. 5—7. Also however, there are *sins of omission.* Usually we find these easier to ignore internally, but God takes these sins just as seriously. This happens when God asks you to do something or to help Him somehow and you refuse. "Anyone, then, who knows the good he ought to do and doesn't do it, sins" (James 4:17).

David embodied the fact that people who are hiding things are miserable. Have you ever hidden something from a friend or loved one and then just felt like dirt when he or she loved you anyway? You knew that you weren't very lovable, but this person still treated you with kindness.

I had a friend confess to me a failure in his marriage, and he said, "Pastor, I just have to tell my wife." He no longer was able to feel worthy of her love without first dealing with the truth. He felt he just needed to tell the truth or he was going to explode. So he told her the truth, and they are seeking healing together.

And in remembering his story, it seems evident that all of us are wired from birth for confession. We need to confess. I think of the first lie I can remember telling my mom at age four. I don't remember the lie—I just remember the feeling. I was sick to my stomach until I told Mom the truth. My conscience was still tender enough to know that Mom deserved better and that I had done wrong. See—it is confession that rids your spirit of "soul kryptonite."

And the word *confess* literally means to "say the same." In other words, when you confess your sin to God, in all its ugliness, you are really just saying what God has already said about it. He says it's wrong in His Word, and you are now calling your particular action or inaction a sin as well. Now you are back on the right side of the truth. You and God are saying the same thing about what you did; that's the essence of confession. David explains the process a little more clearly. He says, "Finally, I confessed all my sins to you and stopped trying to hide them. I said to myself, 'I will confess my rebellion to the LORD.' And you forgave me! All my guilt is gone" (Ps. 32:5, NLT).

The Bible is full of a lot more advice on confession. And its position on confession is that it's a really great deal, because it opens you up to God's favorite thing—love! On this point, I think I like the Catholic sacrament of confession with a priest. Sitting down and telling another human being your sins forces you to think about the possibility that your problem is sin and that by confession you're rid of it. Pascal once said, "Truly it is an evil to be full of faults, but it is still a greater evil to be full of them and to be unwilling to recognize them."[1] Proverbs says, "He who conceals his sins does not prosper, but whoever confesses and renounces them finds mercy" (28:13).

2. Second, we deal with sin when we just accept God's wave of mercy and grace. We can't earn His forgiveness; we just have to learn to take it. "Oh, what joy for those whose rebellion is forgiven, whose sin is put out of sight! Yes, what joy for those whose record the LORD has cleared of sin, whose lives are lived in complete honesty!" (Ps. 32:1-2, NLT).

Once your record with God has been expunged, it's time to live in His strength again. No more wallowing or whining or acting like Harvey Milquetoast. No more hiding or squirming to get away from God. Once you have been forgiven, it's time to rejoice. David said he wasn't going to hide anymore, but instead told God, "You are my hiding place; you protect me from trouble. You surround me with songs of victory" (v. 7, NLT).

It really feels good to come before God free and clear with nothing to hide. It really makes you want to talk with Him more. But confession is only one element of receiving forgiveness. The second is really what makes it stick. Peter tells a group of onlookers that they should "Repent, then, and turn to God, so that your sins may be wiped out, that times of refreshing may come from the Lord" (Acts 3:19-20).

In the original language *repent* simply means "to change one's mind." And if you remember your New Testament, this was Jesus' main message. Quite often He would say, "Repent, for the kingdom of heaven is near" (Matt. 4:17). Change your mind about things—then your actions will change. Repentance and confession must go hand in glove if you are being honest before God. For instance, if you confess a sin that you fully intend to repeat later on tonight, you are not "saying the same" thing about God and "changing your mind" toward that sin. When you change your mind, your behavior always follows.

For instance, in my heart I believe in gravity. I have a certain knowledge that if I jump off a tall building, I will come down with a splat. No more Brett. I have learned over time that gravity always works and that my belief in gravity keeps me off the ledge of the Bank of Oklahoma in downtown Tulsa. But what if I didn't believe in gravity? And what if I had an equally strong urge to put out my arms and fly? Well, I could probably be coerced to jump from said building in the hopes that I could fly like the eagle and soar above the Arkansas River. The point is that what I believe about gravity effects my behavior. And that is why Jesus spent so much time talking with people about what they believe in their hearts, not just how they acted externally.

Author Philip Yancey tells of a conversation he had with a friend who was about to leave his wife for another woman. The man asked Philip, "Do you think God can forgive something as awful as I am about to do?" Yancey paused, because he believes in grace, and drank three cups of coffee before answering. Here's how he responded. It's how I would want to respond to anyone who brought me a similar question. I would love to be as smart as Philip Yancey.

> Can God forgive you? Of course. You know the Bible. God uses murderers and adulterers. . . . Forgiveness is *our* problem, not God's. What we have to go through to commit sin distances us from God—we change in the very act of rebellion—and there's no guarantee we will ever come back. You ask me about forgiveness now, but will you even want it later, especially if it involves repentance?

Yancey says his friend went on to sin and get divorced and that as of yet he hasn't come back to God. He has had to get new friends who approve of his new lifestyle and has forsaken many of his old friends because they just don't understand his new understanding of life.[2]

And here's the really important point to remember. It's one thing to confess your sins to God. But to receive the full benefit and blessing of God, repentance must accompany your confession. When you repent, you acknowledge that your sin is hurting you; you change your mind on the particular issue and understand it is not acceptable behavior for a Christian, and then commit to turn from it for good. Here's probably the most familiar scripture in the Bible about confession. "If we confess our sins, he is faithful and just and will forgive us our sins and purify us from all unrighteousness" (1 John 1:9). I love that promise, don't you.

3. After we have confessed and repented, there is still more to consider. We have to learn to live life following our new pattern of thinking. We have changed our minds—repented—so now what? This is the really cool part. Now God starts pouring out His blessings by guiding us into the future. Once we have called our sin what it is and turned from it, look what happens. "The LORD says, 'I will guide you along the best pathway for your life. I will advise you and watch over you'" (Ps.

32:8, NLT). I think having God as my pilot is one of the most incredible blessings I could ever have. He knows the future, the road ahead, and He's willing to take me down the best path.

I wish I could say I always lived in this blessing as I should, but I haven't. And if I had, I know I would have avoided some of the biggest mistakes in my life. I know God's pathway is the best way—but I get fooled and get stupid. So I was thinking about why this happens to all of us in the faith, and I think it's simple. We don't follow God's guidance because we disengage our faith. We get arrogant, suddenly become clairvoyant, and think we know how to run our lives better than God. And this is the hard part about serving an invisible God: having faith that He is really running things for my good and trusting in Him even though I don't see His face.

But then I was on a plane, and I got to thinking about faith. And I realized that here are some things I do by faith without question. You probably do it too. For instance, when you sit down on a plane heading for Dallas, do you discuss the flight plan with the pilot? Most of the time, do you even see the pilot? How do you really know he or she is up there? How do you really know the pilot knows how to fly a plane? How do you know he or she isn't drunk or high? How do you really know that your plane is going to make it? Well, you and I just exercise a little faith, don't we? Somehow, we give these flawed individuals more faith than we give our great God.

Most of us don't understand how a plane really works, but you know if the ticket says you're going to L.A., chances are good that you'll end up in L.A. (Though not 100 percent of the time!) We simply trust the pilot to get us there. We let him or her drive, because he or she knows how to fly, and we eat the peanuts. (Or on some carriers you now eat nothing and have to like it.)

See—there are certain things we just do by faith. So why is it we won't let God's Word guide our lives? I mean, He has never failed anybody. He never has a crash. He is totally trustworthy. But maybe you say, "Well, I can't see God, so I don't know where He wants me to go." And sometimes that feels true, but I know this much. If you listen and do what is in His Word, you don't have to know how you are going to get to point B. It is God's job to get you there. Just sit down and do what He tells you, and I guarantee that you'll make it.

That's why reading God's Word becomes such a big deal. When you're reading, the God of the universe is guiding the way you think. You're now learning His flight plan for your life. It provides you the guidance that will help you make the kingdom of God a reality here on earth and later in heaven. God is your pilot in life, and He will advise you and watch over you. Isn't that great news?

4. So if we call our sin what it really is, and we accept His mercy and grace and learn to live under His guiding hand to keep us out of trouble and on His path, there's one last step in dealing with sin. And that is when we **learn to live in the *now* and in the *new*.** "Many sorrows come to the wicked, but unfailing love surrounds those who trust the LORD. So rejoice in the LORD and be glad, all you who obey him! Shout for joy, all you whose hearts are pure!" (Ps. 32:10-11, NLT).

Those who have been forgiven and are walking a healthy path in life really have something to shout about. They are living in true freedom. Now I know in some groups shouting is not in vogue, but I think shouting as an act of worship can be pretty cool. After all, when I go to an Oklahoma Sooners football game, I shout a lot.

And come to think of it, David would not have felt very comfortable in any place where you couldn't shout about God's love. Why do some churches seem to act as if the only shout you can let out in worship must be done in four-part harmony? (I'm currently thinking about creating a "bring the shout back into worship" club.) When we learn to live in the now and in the new, we don't want to go back to the old life. Freedom feels too good to let it go, and true joy expressed in worship is our new lifeblood.

When Clark Kent is free from kryptonite, he can do anything. He can right wrongs and foil the plans of the enemy. He's Superman. And I keep thinking, what if God's Church would deal correctly with sin, what good things would be possible? What social and moral evils would be destroyed by people whose lives were lived in total honesty before God?

The good news is that as long as you have breath, you can do what God wants done with the sin in your life. And if you will give it to God and accept His mercy and grace, anything is possible. Take a look at the guy in the next chapter. His story is a grace-and-mercy-from-God highlight film. You won't believe his story!

8

THE COMEBACK KID

Manasseh's Story

Do you think anyone is going to be able to drive a wedge between us and Christ's love for us? There is no way! (Rom. 8:35, TM)

I was a big fan of the lowly Cleveland Browns in the late 1970s and early 1980s, when my hero, Brian Sipe, was the quarterback. Brian Sipe was a guy most people passed over. He was not the NFL prototype. He was too short to play quarterback, 5'10", and he had a weak arm as far as pros go. But in Cleveland during this short window of time, Brian Sipe got to be a star. In 1980, he led the Browns to numerous wins where it appeared that a loss was certain.

That year the Browns became known as the Kardiac Kids because of their late-game heroics. The fan base was mobilized to cheer for all 60 minutes because the Browns were never out of the game, regardless of the score. The Browns did eventually lose to the evil Oakland Raiders in the playoffs, however, but Brian Sipe was still the rags to riches MVP that year. And it was the only year he ever went to a pro bowl. If you ask any Browns fan over 40, they will talk about the golden age of Browns football and the Kardiac Kids.

I was thinking the other day about why God wired us this way. We seem born to identify with the rags-to-riches stories. Everyone outside my home state of Oklahoma enjoyed watching the tiny football team from Boise State beat the mighty Sooners in the 2007 Fiesta Bowl. It was billed as a David vs. Goliath matchup, and once again, David won. (As a biblical scholar, I knew my team was in trouble when they called us Goliath.)

Generations have found great enjoyment in tales like *The Lord of the Rings*, *Cinderella*, *Annie*, and *Oliver Twist*—the kinds of stories that open with a central figure who has nothing, then with a twist of fate, hard work, and so on, makes his or her way out of poverty and bursts onto the scene as the hero. Great fairy tales are born out of our desire for the weak to become strong and for justice to come to the oppressed and burdened. We just want the folks who are down to get up. (And for those who will never be able to get up, we invented the Clapper.) The desire to cheer for redemption is written deeply within the human heart.

But what about the riches-to-rags-to-riches stories? Like in *The Lord of the Rings*, we see a character known as Strider.[1] Strider is really Aragorn, the king of Gondor, if he wants to be king, that is. But Strider chooses to live beneath his rank and chooses a life path that is less than it should have been. The story begins to draw us in as Aragorn finally realizes that he must accept his destiny and become what he was born to be. He goes from riches as a prince to rags and back to riches as the king. This is a little bit like what we do to our celebrities. The media builds them up and then tears them down, only to hope that there is a comeback in the works. In the entertainment industry, actor John Travolta has lived a "rags to riches to rags to riches" existence in the world of movie stardom like few others. And today he is one of the most trusted voices in Hollywood. Why? Well, one reason may be that he's been down a lot and up a lot too. People love a lovable loser, especially when he or she turns the tables and wins.

Jesus knew what made people tick, and He could really tell a story. He knew that a story was the best way to get a truth to stick. He told a story one day about a comeback kid. You may know him as the prodigal son or the lost son, but his story still grips us every time we hear it. The story hinges on a young man with a great inheritance and a great father. He asks his father for his share of the estate, now instead of later. And since the father seems to have missed the course on tough love, he willingly obliges.

The young man goes to the Vegas of his day, and he quickly loses everything. He ends up in rags, feeding the hogs, and his mind drifts toward home. And you likely know the rest of the story, about how he goes home hoping for an hourly job but instead is greeted by a lovesick, generous father who decides to bless him with a party instead of a lecture on money management. The story says a lot about the father, how he loves in spite of his son's shortcomings, and that was one of Jesus' points.

But stories about other comeback kids are equally compelling to me. I can think of another young man who was possibly the prototype for this character that Jesus was talking about. Although Jesus didn't mention him in the story, I think He may have been thinking about him in the back of His mind. Jesus loved a good comeback story, and there's no comeback story any more compelling than the story of a young man named Manasseh.

Manasseh's story is told to us in the Old Testament Book of 2 Kings, and notice it begins rather benignly. "Manasseh was twelve years old when he became king, and he reigned in Jerusalem fifty-five years" (21:1). I once heard Robert Schuller deliver a sermon in which all his points rhymed. I thought it was cool, so I came up with this to sum up the life of the real Comeback Kid, King Manasseh.

King Manasseh was "evil displayed."

And by his actions God's people were swayed.

God spoke a word, but they still disobeyed.

As a result of their sin, a great price would be paid.

But by God's grace a new course could be laid.

OK, not very impressive I know, but it still rhymes, and that's half the battle of poetry in my mind.

So let me set the stage historically before I take my poem apart, line by line. Manasseh is only 12 years old when he takes the lead of God's nation. And he is following in his father Hezekiah's footsteps. If you don't remember your Old Testament history, here's a quick summary.

After King David established Israel's greatness, his son King Solomon led Israel toward expansion. This expansion moved faster than Solomon's ability to keep pace. He then led this nation to the brink of disaster, which came on the heels of many questionable moral practices and forced labor conscription that were not at all good for God's people. After his death, the embittered people took opposing sides. After a civil war, Israel was torn into two pieces—Israel to the north and Judah to the south. Israel was pretty much a wicked mess most of the time, and Judah was usually marginally better. For both kingdoms, their wickedness usually involved idol worship and the practices associated with it. And with the wickedness came God's wrath and a withdrawal of His hand of blessing.

Manasseh was now king over Judah. And Judah was in the middle of a great comeback. Hezekiah had been a righteous king. In football terms, it was the fourth quarter, and John Elway (nemesis of the Cleveland Browns) had just thrown three touchdown passes to bring his team back from the brink of defeat. Judah had momentum and God was moving on their behalf. Things were finally looking good again for Judah after decades of sin. Hezekiah had cleaned house, literally. Look at his list of accomplishments.

> [Hezekiah] removed the high places, smashed

> the sacred stones and cut down the Asherah poles. He broke into pieces the bronze snake Moses had made, for up to that time the Israelites had been burning incense to it. (It was called Nehushtan.) Hezekiah trusted in the LORD, the God of Israel. There was no one like him among all the kings of Judah, either before him or after him. He held fast to the LORD and did not cease to follow him; he kept the commands the LORD had given Moses. And the LORD was with him; he was successful in whatever he undertook *(2 Kings 18:4-7)*.

Hezekiah got God's house in order, removed the idols, and lived successfully. All of Judah's problems seemed to be solved. But Hezekiah died, and now Manasseh had his shot at greatness.

King Manasseh Was "Evil Displayed"

Manasseh had the longest reign, 55 years, of any king of Judah. Now compare his list of accomplishments with those of his father. "He did evil in the eyes of the LORD" (21:2). The first thing that the Bible says about his reign was that he did evil. Then he went and undid all the great things his father had done. But like the infomercial for the Pocket Fisherman, I can say to you, "But wait—there's more."

> He built altars in the temple of the LORD, of which the LORD had said, "In Jerusalem I will put my Name." In both courts of the temple of the LORD, he built altars to all the starry hosts. He sacrificed his own son in the fire, practiced sorcery and divination, and consulted mediums and spiritists. He did much evil in the eyes of the LORD, provoking him to anger *(vv. 4-6).*

The picture is quickly going downhill. Manasseh practiced witchcraft, sorcery, and divination, erected idols in God's Temple, and sacrificed his son in a fiery ceremony of wickedness. Manasseh certainly may have felt at home in today's Hollywood scene, but he didn't fit at all as a leader of God's people. One of the things I ponder when looking at this story is how all of this garbage got started again. I mean, anybody with any kind of knowledge of Judah's history could tell you how a righteous king brings honor on his nation and vice-versa.

So how did it all get started again? At age 12, Manasseh was old enough to realize what his father had done. He was likely very schooled in the oral history of his people. He would have gotten the best in education. He also knew of the power of the Lord. He had to have seen it up close in the Temple. Maybe it was just a little bit of teenage rebellion combined with too much power that tipped the scales—the same thing that happens to kids who grow up in church today. They want to take a short trip to the wild side. Nothing too evil, mind you, just a little bad stuff that their parents have kept them from over the years. And with Dad dead, Manasseh had nobody to call when he stayed out too late. The results were frightening no matter how innocently it started.

Manasseh may have fallen prey to their version of political correctness. He was probably coached to see both sides of this sin vs. righteousness issue and may have been taught that you shouldn't be too hard on those pagans who live around here and their foreign gods. (In fact, he may have been prodded to drop the word *pagans* altogether, since that may have hurt their feelings.) Manasseh was likely a free thinker who would chide us today to understand our terrorists and not judge those too harshly who strap bombs to their chest in the name of their faith. If they feel it is right for them, then obviously, it is. Right and wrong were probably no longer issues for Manasseh. Moral relativism is not a new phenomenon. It is simply a retread of common thinking since the Fall among those who lack the courage to seek the real truth or the backbone to stand by it when truth is challenged.

I am frightened at how quickly this kind of thinking has taken root in our nation and schools (even those called Christian schools). People are told that it's judgmental and harsh to speak the truth about sin. And it seems that many educators and civic leaders walk on eggshells while the world floats down Sin River.

But Manasseh's walk on the wild side didn't stop at first base. He was the most detestable king that Judah ever had. "He has done more evil than the Amorites who preceded him and has led Judah into sin with his idols" (v. 11). He was no ordinary sinner—he was horrible.

By His Actions, God's People Were Swayed

Not only did Manasseh practice evil, but he misled God's people to do the same. "Thus Manasseh misled Judah and the inhabitants of Jerusalem to do more evil than the nations whom the LORD destroyed before the sons of Israel" (2 Chron. 33:9, NASB).

Now, the use of the word *misled* means he didn't lead right but wrong. His intent was to pull people into his way of life and away from his father's. This is the *negative side* of "having community." The positive side is seen in the Body of Christ where each person supports one another for his or her good. *The negative side of community is that when sin starts in a community and goes unchecked, it can catch fire quickly.* Deep inside, everyone knows it's no fun to sin all alone. And since people are communal by nature, it's tons more fun to have group sin. It somehow makes us feel insulated from guilt. And the deeper the sin became, for Judah, the easier it got to ignore the fuddy-duddies of previous generations.

Let me comment here on one of the dangers I see happening in our American culture. We seem to elevate youthfulness and discard aged wisdom. Plastic surgeons are carving up people as fast as they can sign them up. The success of makeover TV shows tells us that saggy skin and wrinkles are no longer seen as a normal life cycle occurrence. Anything to stay young is the motto most have adopted.

But there is a devilish notion at work here. When we elevate youthfulness, we also elevate foolishness, because young people usually do dumb things (including me). And if the only heroes in pop culture are under 30, then the only voices our kids are hearing are those unseasoned by the mistakes of life. Voices of reason get pushed to the fringe as those who are not progressive or out of touch.

What's worse is that youth gets elevated in the church as well. I have heard of churches searching for pastors using the criterion that "we want somebody under 40." OK, that seems smart if you're building a football team, but not a church. Now, there's nothing noble about being stuck in time and afraid of trying new things. But *youth* doesn't necessarily mean *good.* In the church especially, we ought to set the tone that age is not the most important criteria of leadership but rather character and love. End of soapbox.

Back to group sin. The apostle Paul understood the communal nature of sin when he dealt with the church at Corinth. He knew that if you hang out very long with a sinner who claims to be a God follower, you are more likely to resemble that person than turn him or her back around. He said, "You are not to associate with anyone who claims to be a Christian yet indulges in sexual sin, or is greedy, or worships idols, or is abusive, or a drunkard, or a swindler. Don't even eat with such people" (1 Cor. 5:11, NLT). Sin spreads and sin destroys, especially when sin happens in leadership.

The Manasseh story just illustrates for us the appeal of sin for each generation. Sin is nothing new, and neither are the consequences. In the opening chapter of this book, we took a look at Israel after Joshua died. They began to chase after other gods. And here we see the broken nation of Israel, still bumping their heads on the idols of their day.

God Spoke a Word, but They Still Disobeyed

So the prophets spoke up for God, but the people

were already hardened to His voice. The prophets had seen enough, and God was prompting them to deliver a well-timed message. "The LORD spoke to Manasseh and his people, but they paid no attention" (2 Chron. 33:10, NASB).

Ouch! Nothing hurts a prophet's self-esteem like people who don't pay attention. Since I get to preach every week, I am well acquainted with the posture of those who are listening and those who are just punching a holy time card each week and thinking of something else. Well, actually, it's easier to see if they are listening by how they live. And evidently, the people were not going to change. The effects of group sin had taken hold. Their hearts were hardened, and not even God's voice would penetrate.

Hardening is so sad to see. I remember one of my friends in high school experienced hardening. One year he was a model citizen, trying to do the right thing. His conscience was tender. But over the course of one school year, he got in with the wrong crowd and began using and selling drugs. It was weird, because even his countenance changed. He started to look older and meaner. He seemed more suspicious of others and lacked the joy he used to have. He lost a ton of weight and began to look more and more as if he wouldn't break the power of darkness on his life.

I think hardening is the scariest part of group sin. Paul talked about the way this happens: "For although they knew God, they neither glorified him as God nor gave thanks to him, but their thinking became futile and their foolish hearts were darkened" (Rom. 1:21).

This is a really troubling scripture, because he is talking about people that know God. And these same people, just like Judah before, begin to go down a very dangerous road. Look how God chooses to respond to group disobedience among His people.

"Therefore God gave them over in the sinful desires of their hearts to sexual impurity for the degrading of their bodies with one another. They exchanged the truth of God for a lie" (vv. 24-25). "God gave them over." I don't really like that phrase. I like the parts in the Bible where God protects me from myself and others. I don't like the idea of God giving me over to my own stupid desires. Yet this is what happens when your heart hardens and you start to live by dark thinking. The Word of God, the truth, just doesn't get through like it used to. You may still go to church and listen to sermons on tape. You can be a Sunday School teacher, board member, deacon, or even a pastor and still exchange the truth for a lie. God can be speaking, but if you don't listen, your hearing just keeps getting worse. And then you get involved in doing really stupid things that hurt a lot of people. When people of God begin a pattern of willful sin, watch out.

"Furthermore, since they did not think it worthwhile to retain the knowledge of God, he gave them over to a depraved mind, to do what ought not to be done" (v. 28). Those words *depraved mind* really scare me. The word *depraved* makes me think of people like serial killer Ted Bundy, Charles Manson, Hannibal Lecter, or somebody crazy. But certainly not about Sally Jo who sits on the second row at First Church. Paul knew that the craziness we see exhibited on the outside of some people is within us all if we let it. Manasseh led the people of Judah to exchange the truth of God for living a lie. And it would get worse before it got better.

God's Word always demands a response. When we choose to agree with His Word, we walk in the light and grow in grace. When we reject His Word, we walk in darkness and become more easily deceived.

As a Result of Sin, a Great Price Would Be Paid

There's always a payday, isn't there? Sin always costs more than you want to spend. On the Internet the other day I was searching for the address of a friend of mine who is in prison. He was convicted of murder in 1987, and I hadn't heard from him in nearly 20 years.

He was my youth group sponsor at church, and he was always good to us, so I wanted to write him a note of thanks and encouragement. So I was surfing the Texas Department of Criminal Justice Web site, and I stumbled across the last statements of some offenders prior to their execution. As I surveyed these statements, most were penitent and some were still angry, and others were still saying that they were innocent. I was drawn to statements made by the penitent. Sin always carries a heavy price tag.

November 15, 2005, the last statement of Robert Dale Rowell: "Yes sir. I would like to apologize to the victim's family and all the grief I have caused them. I would like to say I love the girls next to them. Praise the Lord. Let's go, Warden. That's it."[2]

May 19, 2005, the last statement of Richard Cartwright: "Yes, I do. I just want to thank all my friends and family who gave me support these past eight years. I want to apologize to the victim's family for the pain I caused them."[3]

May 3, 2005, the last statement of Lonnie Pursley: "Yes. I would like to address the victim's family. I received your poem and I am very grateful for your forgiveness. I still want to ask for it anyway. I have Jesus in my heart and I am sorry for any pain I caused you all. Thank you for your forgiveness. I am sorry."[4]

March 8, 2005, the last statement of George Hopper: "I want to apologize to you, and I am sorry. I have made a lot of mistakes in my life. The things I did changed so many lives. I can't take it back, it was an atrocity. I am sorry. I beg your forgiveness, I know I am not worthy of it. I love you, Mom and Dad, and all my family. Thank you for everything. Jesus, thank you for your love and saving grace. Thank you for shedding your blood on Calvary for me. Thank you, Jesus, for the love you have shown me."[5]

Those are four men who knew the cost of sin. And they were people just like you and me. They once had a future and hopes and dreams. But poor decisions led to hardening, and hardening led to death. Sin creates a wasted life.

God gave Manasseh a chance by speaking through the prophets. But he didn't listen. So God did what God does. He let sin take its natural course of destruction. "So the LORD brought against them the army commanders of the king of Assyria, who took Manasseh prisoner, put a hook in his nose, bound him with bronze shackles and took him to Babylon" (2 Chron. 33:11).

There's a saying that "we can choose our own way, but we can't choose the consequences." A hook in his nose was not what Manasseh had in mind when he put the idols up in the Temple. He never considered that his actions may have consequences. But there he went.

In listening to the stories of corporate greed that have abounded this decade, you see this principle is still pretty common. The Enron story has been center stage in the media over the past few years. The leadership at Enron lied to investors about the huge losses and then tried to cover it up, while still lining their own pockets. Somehow they forgot to consider the consequences if they ever got caught. Sin makes you feel invincible sometimes. But the damage to the families of Houston has been done.

> Thousands of Enron employees lost their life savings after Enron collapsed. A lawsuit on the behalf of a group of Enron's shareholders has been filed against Enron executives and directors. This lawsuit accuses twenty-nine of these executives and directors of insider trading and misleading the public. Thousands of Enron employees and investors lost their life savings, kids' college funds, and pensions when Enron collapsed.[6]

Sin cost Manasseh a great deal, and it cost his nation as well.

It's interesting to note that in the Book of 2 Kings, the writer doesn't tell us everything that the writer of 2 Chronicles does. Kings tells of Manasseh's death after a life of sin. He doesn't mention the part about being led away to Babylon and what followed. I'm not sure why—he didn't say anything. But I'm glad that the writer of the Chronicles adds one of the greatest lines in all of the Old Testament.

By God's Grace, a New Course Is Laid

Look what Manasseh does when he learns the jig is up. "In his distress he sought the favor of the LORD his God and humbled himself greatly before the God of his fathers. And when he prayed to him, the LORD was moved by his entreaty and listened to his plea; so he brought him back to Jerusalem and to his kingdom. Then Manasseh knew that the LORD is God" (2 Chron. 33:12-13).

Wow! Talk about a comeback of biblical proportions. Manasseh was out of the game, he had been removed from power, and a bigger team now had the lead. And if I were God, which we are all thankful isn't the case, I wouldn't be so inclined to listen to this guy. After all, he deserved to rot for a while. After everything he had done, he needed to pay. But God sees things differently. The Bible says, "The LORD was moved by his entreaty and listened to his plea."

Starting to see the picture of the father in the story

of the prodigal son? (Hint: It's the same guy doing the forgiving here.) Can you believe what God will put up with just to get things right with His kids? Can you believe the extent of His mercy and grace to all of us who don't deserve it? This is the heart of the gospel message. David once wrote it like this, "Oh, give thanks to the LORD, for He is good! For His mercy endures forever" (1 Chron. 16:34, NKJV).

After reading that story and seeing this ending, I get chill bumps all over me. I'm just amazed at how much God loves His fallen children regardless of their history.

I'm convinced that most of the world doesn't know these kinds of stories about God. They picture God as a gentle old grandpa or a cosmic quitter who started the world but couldn't figure out how to run it or like a mean God in the vein of Greek mythology or as one who is too busy to care about any of us little people.

Maybe they picture Him only as a lawgiver who is waiting for people to mess up so He can give them what they deserve. And really, within the Christian Church, this is the picture most of us grow up with. We are trained to perform for God rather than relate to Him. And when we see our life as Christians as being a performance for God, our spiritual life centers on dos and don'ts. We gauge our faith on how many minutes we spend doing godly things rather than how deep our connection goes with Him.

Manasseh's story is a story about God. And once he realized the true nature of his God, Manasseh gladly made some changes to complete the comeback. And as you look at all he did following his conversion experience, know that this is the path we can take to keep us from going back after the god of cool.

> Afterward he rebuilt the outer wall of the City of David, west of the Gihon spring in the valley, as far as the entrance of the Fish Gate and encircling the hill of Ophel; he also made it much higher. He stationed military commanders in all the fortified cities in Judah.
>
> He got rid of the foreign gods and removed the image from the temple of the LORD, as well as all the altars he had built on the temple hill and in Jerusalem; and he threw them out of the city. Then he restored the altar of the LORD and sacrificed fellowship offerings and thank offerings on it, and told Judah to serve the LORD, the God of Israel. The people, however, continued to sacrifice at the high places, but only to the LORD their God *(2 Chron. 33:14-17)*.

Manasseh starts acting like his dad by cleaning house. First, he puts the walls up again, but this time higher than ever. This scripture will preach, as this should be our story as well. If you have fallen to a particular temptation over and over and want to keep from going that way again, you have to keep your walls high.

My friend Buddy leads a ministry called Celebrate Recovery. He deals with folks who are tired of living a life chained to sins caused by addiction, codependence, compulsive behaviors, and so on. They get free from their sin by God's grace and with the help of others. He tells me that recovering drug addicts have to keep their walls up high or they relapse every time. He says there are certain things that are triggers for the addiction. Like for alcoholics, the holidays are a big trigger, because they always used to drink a lot during the holidays. So our Celebrate Recovery meeting helps them from having to think about the holidays as they used to and gives them friends who are trying to stay sober as well.

Certain places also trigger sin. For the Internet porn addict, the trigger is being online in an empty room with no safeguards in place. The person must learn to stay off-line in vulnerable places and build the walls higher than the enemy can climb. So the recovery process is all about building walls between you and the triggers. Manasseh did that.

Manasseh also got rid of the filth from his past. All the paraphernalia that would remind him of other gods had to go. So many people forget this part of coming to Christ. They want to bring Jesus to their mess and hope that they all get along. Manasseh makes amends with God and leads others to do the same. Manasseh knew the power of evil, and he knew his own weakness when it came to sin. He knew that sin was not something you could afford to play with, so he got rid of the hindrances.

One of my favorite Bible verses talks about the process Manasseh went through:

> Therefore, since we are surrounded by such a great cloud of witnesses, let us throw off everything that hinders and the sin that so easily entangles, and let us run with perseverance the race marked out for us. Let us fix our eyes on Jesus, the author and perfecter of our faith, who for the joy set before him endured the cross, scorning its shame, and sat down at the right hand of the throne of God *(Heb. 12:1-2)*.

This is our invitation into the holy life. This is our summons to travel light and pursue Christ and run a race that matters. They tell me that marathon runners have to keep a picture of the finish line in their head to keep their legs going in the right direction during their grueling 26-mile trek. (Due to conscientious objection, I would not be in that group.) Somehow seeing the goal gives them strength.

God has a course for your life to take and things He would like you to do. And the only way you can accomplish all of those things for God is to have your focus on Christ. To focus on Christ, you have to learn to travel light. And that's really what this book has been all about. It's been aimed at helping you learn more about the hindrances and entanglements that slow down your race by identifying attitudes that are hard to spot in any of us. But if you will choose Christ and pursue Him with all you have, then the lure of cool will take its place in the pile of things that you have tossed aside in order to travel light.

Whether your life resembles Manasseh, the prodigal son, or somebody not so bad yet, God is the same. He is rooting for you and longing for you to humble your heart and begin a pursuit with real rewards.

9

REDEFINING A NEW KIND OF COOL

Delight yourself in the L*ORD and he will give you the desires of your heart* (Ps. 37:4).

It's really funny to me that I'm writing a book. My editor can likely attest to the fact that English was always on the bottom of my "classes in school I really enjoyed" list. I just had a hard time ciphering sentence diagrams and understanding the difference between an adverb and an adjective. I was a *Star Trek* fan, so I grew up hearing the great split infinitive, issued by Capt. James T. Kirk at the beginning of every episode. Even if you are far from a "trekkie," you have likely heard his phrase "to reach new galaxies, to explore new worlds, *to boldly go* where no man has gone before." English teachers don't like it when you put *boldly* in the middle of their infinitive "to go." It just irritates them. Maybe it was just me, but did you ever notice that English teachers were always irritated about something that nobody else was too upset about?

I'm not an English major, but I have noticed something about languages in general. Every language has this neat habit of redefining words over time. It usually starts by using a common word in a slang kind of way. For instance, the term *cool* should refer to temperature or color. But somewhere back in time, a beatnik poet somewhere decided to make *cool* a term that *Merriam-Webster* says is "**a** : very good : EXCELLENT; *also* : ALL RIGHT **b** : FASHIONABLE, HIP."[1] So, since beatnik poets can redefine a good word, I figure an out-of-touch pastor should get a shot at it too.

Here's my thought. We need to redefine *cool* by adding a *name.* English teachers would call this personification. And in my mind, nobody personifies the slang term *cool* better than Jesus. And if we had a real picture of Jesus—not the blond-haired, blue-eyed Jesus but the rugged, Middle Eastern Jesus—He should be in the book next to the definition for *cool.* We just need to redefine *cool* in light of the Light of the World. Think about it. Jesus is the King of cool.

What He says and does in the Bible is cool. He always makes the religious establishment uncomfortable and sides with the fringe. (The establishment is never cool.) Hippies in the 1960s liked Jesus because of that, and many of them even named themselves "Jesus people" after finding Him.

How He loves the unlovable is cool. Nobody knew this kind of cool better than the lying, cheating, friendless tax collector Zacchaeus. In the real world he was the guy most likely to be left out of the party, every party. But in the cool world of Jesus he got to host a meal for the King of the Universe. Wow! (I'm guessing that Jesus probably would've liked English teachers too.)

How Jesus heals people is really cool too. A blind man named Bartimaeus thought so. Let me start the story. Jesus and His posse were leaving town on foot and walked right by Bart, and Bart yelled at Jesus to get His attention. Let's pick it up in Mark 10:

> "Be quiet!" some of the people yelled at him. But he only shouted louder, "Son of David, have mercy on me!" When Jesus heard him, he stopped and said, "Tell him to come here." So they called

> the blind man. "Cheer up," they said. "Come on, he's calling you!" Bartimaeus threw aside his coat, jumped up, and came to Jesus. "What do you want me to do for you?" Jesus asked. "Teacher," the blind man said, "I want to see!" And Jesus said to him, *"Go your way. Your faith has healed you."* And instantly the blind man could see! Then he followed Jesus down the road *(vv. 48-52,* NLT*, emphasis added).*

Bart asked for sight, and he got it. How cool is that? I simply can't imagine what it would be like to get sight after being blind. I have no understanding of blindness. I mean, I've been in a dark room where I couldn't see my hand in front of my face, but I usually had the option of flicking a switch to cure it. This guy had no cure, and he had no light. He was relegated to a life of brutal reliance on the goodness and guilty consciences of others who passed by. And since the towns back then were pretty small and the roads pretty narrow, everybody had seen this guy for as long as they could remember. But then he saw *the* Light, literally. And the cool part is that he knew what to do next. He *followed* the Light.

Can I speak to pastors for a second? I think at this point many leaders in the Evangelical Church world have missed it. They want to see numerical results (which can sometimes become idols in and of themselves), so they stress the conversion or healing moment and not the part that says "then he followed . . ." I'm thinking that Jesus thought the following part was the most important, that it was the goal of the conversion or healing.

It is always interesting to me how Jesus tried to get away from crowds and how He kept narrowing the field with comments about the narrow gate and how His followers must "eat [his] flesh . . . and drink his blood" (John 6:53). Jesus apparently didn't do low-commitment evangelism very well. (In fact, He was a little insensitive, don't you think?) I know of some large churches that purposely refuse to ask anything difficult of their people so that it will be a "safe place" to worship for the unbeliever. How have we turned the process of discipleship into an optional accessory to our faith, if we have the time or the stomach for it? In his book *The Great Omission*, my literary hero Dallas Willard expands on this question and gives great application for those of us attempting to teach a generation raised on American easy-believism. I plan on getting a house near Dallas in heaven if possible.

And on that subject, do you remember how Jesus gave an altar call? "And Jesus said to them, 'Follow Me, and I will make you become fishers of men.' Immediately they left their nets and followed Him" (Mark 1:17-18, NASB).

Later He added the words "take up your cross" (Matt. 10:38) to the "follow me" command. Cross-carrying has never been a beginner's sport, but apparently that's what He hands us when we sign up for His team. At least that's what He says. Others may disagree.

Bartimaeus thought eyesight was cool—so much so that it was natural that he would find a way to follow the One who gave it to him. I wonder what kind of cross Bartimaeus carried in his lifetime after meeting Jesus.

Jesus is so cool. How He still rescues; how He still heals; how He takes the broken pieces of a once broken life; and how He puts it all together like an artist, fashioning colored glass shards into a stained-glass window—that is cool! I think stained glass is one of the greatest symbols in the Christian faith because it so well describes what happens when His light shines through our brokenness.

Only Jesus can change a human heart, nobody else. And when He sets up shop in your heart, you will never want another master. Jesus is the coolest.

I enjoy talking to people with big jolly voices like Bartimaeus probably had. I look forward to meeting him in heaven, hearing that bellowing voice that struck a chord with the heart of the Master that day on His walk down the road. I'm partial to big voices because my father Norman owns one of the loudest singing voices I've ever heard. When he sings at church you can hear him, on key mind you, above everybody else. I love to hear my dad worshiping God because it comes from his huge heart. He loves Jesus and he and Bart will likely be good buds someday. I also have another friend named Brad who used to be a DJ. I call him the human microphone because his voice vibrates through concrete walls.

Jesus probably had a big voice too. His voice went through rock. When He called Lazarus from the grave and told him to get up after being dead for four days, Lazarus got up. That was cool. Can you tell that I'm writing faster and faster as I talk about Jesus? I just can't wait to see Him face-to-face!

Let me change the scenery for a minute. Bartimaeus received his sight from Jesus, but another guy was struck blind by Jesus when He appeared to him in a vision. A little sci-fi, I know, but still really cool. The man's name was Saul, and if you know the Bible, you know that one day he was on his way from Jerusalem to Damascus to help destroy this thing that would soon be known as Christianity. Saul was a good Jew, but he didn't know Jesus. All he knew was that this Jesus thing was getting totally out of control and that he and his buddies had to do something to stop it. He was really sincere in his religion—but sincerely wrong.

So he's on the road and a bright light shines and it knocks him off his horse. He sees Jesus, and Jesus asks him why he's persecuting Him (Acts 9). Saul is blinded by this encounter. I guess Jesus likes to do things differently every now and again. Jesus tells Saul to go to town and that when he gets there, he will get instructions. Saul complies, and he goes to the house of a Christian named Ananias. Ananias prays for him, and Jesus heals him and restores his sight and fills him with His Spirit. And just like Bartimaeus, Saul changes the way he sees things. He now sees in a different way. While a persecutor, he was blind to the reality of Jesus. But now as a Christ follower he sets his sights on his Healer and never changes course. The Truth had set him free. So look at what he did next. "Saul stayed with the believers in Damascus for a few days. And immediately he began preaching about Jesus in the synagogues, saying, 'He is indeed the Son of God!'" (v. 20, NLT).

I mean, the scales had barely hit the floor and Saul had changed his tune. He couldn't shut up about how great Jesus was. He was on fire. Why is this not happening as much today?

Sometimes I wonder when people say they struggle sharing their faith in Jesus with other people. They say they aren't sure what to say or are embarrassed or the sun got in their eyes or they had a toothache or—you name the excuse. It makes me wonder if they have really met Jesus. The angels must watch us and sit around shaking their heads. How can we be so timid about this great gift?

I mean, if you see a great movie or last week's episode of *American Idol,* you don't have a hard time telling your friends about it, do you? And if you meet a famous entertainer or athlete, everybody in your inner circle would hear every detail, right? I mean if George Bush or Bill Clinton were to sit down for dinner at the Rickey house, I guarantee the digital photos of me and "W" or me and Bubba would be all over the Internet. I would tell everybody who would listen about who came to my house, who still got stuff stuck in his teeth, and who ate with his mouth open like everybody else at times. Same would be true of you, I would guess.

Saul was a person of sight but not able to see. Then he was blinded by the light but was able to finally really see. Then after he was able to see, he shared what he saw with others. A good case of *real* Christianity, you could say. Cool stuff.

After Saul got new eyesight, God gave him the name Paul. And He would use Paul to start churches all over the place. This whole name change deal is really cool—kind of like when Jesus changed Simon's name to Rocky (Peter). Have you ever noticed that only cool people can give a nickname that sticks?

Both Peter and Paul were able to stay away from the lure of other allegiances and stay true to Jesus. They were both able to finish strong and were eventually martyred for their confession. Their example still serves as a tremendous model for all of us walking this out today. So how did they keep their spiritual vision when everything was screaming at them to drop it? Can we really do the same thing in the new millennium given the additional temptations that had never even entered the minds of these two Christ followers?

Listen to how Paul stayed focused near the end of his life. He said, "Friends, don't get me wrong: By no means do I count myself an expert in all of this, but I've got my eye on the goal, where God is beckoning us onward—to Jesus. I'm off and running, and I'm not turning back" (Phil. 3:13-14, TM). Paul said, "I'm off and running"—I'm chasing a life that really matters.

So how about you? Are you able to say that today? Since you have read this book to these final pages, I believe that God may be using these words to speak to you on a bunch of different levels. My prayer for you is that you will have your true goal in life marked out with crystal clarity and that your goal will be a name; that your goal will be Jesus.

So now that we have redefined *cool* in light of God's Word, I do hereby give you full permission to begin to chase cool. He is truly beautiful and this pursuit won't leave you empty, it will keep you full. You will know Him when you get Him. He doesn't try to hide. He is available to any who will really look and truly respond to His captivating voice. And when you find Him, you will tell others because you will want them to know what you know and to feel what you feel. So go ahead, take off, and let the eternal chase begin.

NOTES

Chapter 1

1. Charles Colson and Harold Fickett, *The Good Life* (Wheaton, Ill.: Tyndale House Publishers, 2005), xiv-xv.

2. A conversation with Dr. Shelton from Southern Nazarene University, 1983.

3. Steve Farber, "P. Diddy Makes Sean John Rims for Luxury SUV's, Trucks, and Cars," *Articles.Web.Com*, http://www.articles.web.com/Article/P--Diddy-Makes-Sean-John-Rims-For-Luxury-SUV-s--Trucks--And-Cars-/13223 (accessed July 11, 2007).

4. Gary Ruskin, "Why They Whine: How Corporations Prey on Children," *Mothering Magazine* (November/December 1999), 42.

5. David G. Myers, "Wealth, Well-Being, and the New American Dream," *Enough: A Quarterly Report on Consumption, the Quality of Life and the Environment*, no. 12 (Summer 2000): 5.

Chapter 2

1. Donald Miller, *Blue like Jazz* (Nashville: Thomas Nelson, 2003), 106.

2. Ibid., 107.

3. Christine Sine and Tom Sine, *Living on Purpose* (Grand Rapids: Baker Books, 2002), 31.

Chapter 5

1. Erwin McManus, *Seizing Your Divine Moments* (Nashville: Thomas Nelson, 2002), 7-8.

2. Robert W. Burtner and Robert E. Chiles, *John Wesley's Theology* (Nashville: Abingdon Press, 1954), 101-2.

Chapter 6

1. Rick Warren, *The Purpose-Driven Life* (Grand Rapids: Zondervan, 2002).

2. Donald Miller, *Searching for God Knows What* (Nashville: Thomas Nelson Publishers, 2005).

Chapter 7

1. Phillip Yancey, *What's So Amazing About Grace?* (Grand Rapids: Zondervan Publishing House, 1997), 181.

2. Ibid., 180.

Chapter 8

1. J. R. R. Tolkien, *The Lord of the Rings* (Boston: Houghton-Mifflin, 1967).

2. Texas Department of Criminal Justice, http://www.tdcj.state.tx.us/stat/rowellrobertlast.htm (accessed July 11, 2007).

3. Texas Department of Criminal Justice, http://www.tdcj.state.tx.us/stat/cartwrightrichardlast.htm (accessed July 11, 2007).

4. Texas Department of Criminal Justice, http://www.tdcj.state.tx.us/stat/pursleylonnielast.htm (accessed July 11, 2007).

5. Texas Department of Criminal Justice, http://www.tdcj.state.tx.us/stat/hoppergeorgelast.htm (accessed July 11, 2007).

6. *Wikipedia,* s.v. "Enron," http://en.wikipedia.org/wiki/Enron (accessed July 11, 2007).

Chapter 9

1. *Merriam-Webster Online,* s.v. "cool," http://www.mwl.merriam-webster.com/dictionary/cool (accessed July 11, 2007).